THE FALL OF SOVIE
1985–9

C000061150

Studies in European History

Series Editors: John Breuilly
                       Peter Wilson

The Fall of Soviet Communism 1985–91

Jeremy Smith

First published in 2005 by
PALGRAVE MACMILLAN
Houndmills, Basingstoke, Hampshire RG21 6XS and
175 Fifth Avenue, New York, N.Y. 10010
Companies and representatives throughout the world.

PALGRAVE MACMILLAN is the global academic imprint of the Palgrave
Macmillan division of St. Martin's Press, LLC and of Palgrave Macmillan Ltd.
Macmillan ® is a registered trademark in the United States, United Kingdom
and other countries. Palgrave is a registered trademark in the European
Union and other countries.

ISBN-13: 978–1–4039–1602–0 paperback
ISBN-10: 1–4039–1602–0 paperback

This book is printed on paper suitable for recycling and made from fully
managed and sustained forest sources.

A catalogue record for this book is available from the British Library.

A catalog record for this book is available from the Library of Congress.

10 9 8 7 6 5 4 3 2 1
14 13 12 11 10 09 08 07 06 05

Printed in China.

Contents

Contents

Editors' Preface

The Studies in European History series offers a guide to developments in a field of history that has become increasingly specialised with the sheer volume of new research and literature now produced. Each book has three main objectives. The primary purpose is to offer an informed assessment of opinion on a key episode or theme in European history. Second, each title presents a distinct interpretation and conclusions from someone who is closely involved with current debates in the field. Third, it provides students and teachers with a succinct introduction to the topic, with the essential information necessary to understand it and the literature being discussed. Equipped with an annotated bibliography and other aids to study, each book provides an ideal starting point to explore important events and processes that have shaped Europe's history to the present day.

Books in the series introduce students to historical approaches which in some cases are very new and which, in the normal course of things, would take many years to filter down to textbooks. By presenting history's cutting edge, we hope that the series will demonstrate some of the excitement that historians, like scientists, feel as they work on the frontiers of their subject. The series also has an important contribution to make in publicising what historians are doing, and making it accessible to students and scholars in this and related disciplines.

JOHN BREUILLY
PETER H. WILSON

A Note on References

References are cited throughout in brackets according to the numbering in the general bibliography, with page references where necessary indicated by a semi-colon after the bibliography number.

Acknowledgements

I would like to express particular thanks to Ed Bacon, John Breuilly, Phil Hanson and Palgrave's anonymous reviewer for their most helpful comments and corrections on various stages of the manuscript. Any remaining errors are my own. Students on the MA course at the University of Birmingham's Centre for Russian and East European Studies have, over a number of years, helped me identify the historiographical problems with the study of the Gorbachev period, and have suggested ways of overcoming them. I am grateful to all my colleagues at CREES for the stimulating research and writing environment, which is unrivalled in Europe, and which certainly has had an impact on this book. Finally, my wife Hanna and children Saga and Max have had, at times, to tolerate an even more distracted husband and father than usual, and for their support I am eternally grateful.

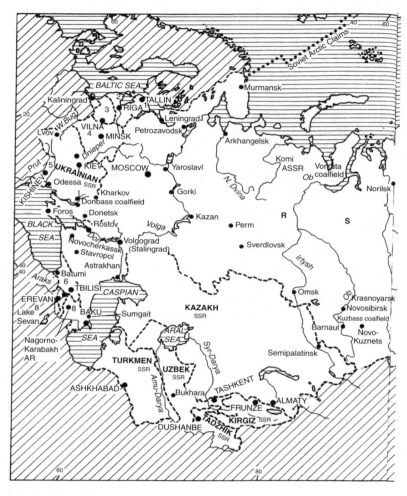

Map 1   The USSR circa 1990

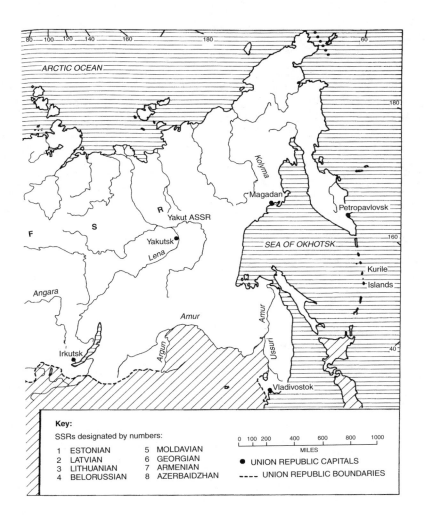

ARCTIC OCEAN

R
S
F

Yakut ASSR

Yakutsk
Lena
Angara
Amur
Argun
Irkutsk

Kolyma
Magadan
Petropavlovsk

SEA OF OKHOTSK

Kurile
Islands

Amur
Ussuri
Vladivostok

Key:

SSRs designated by numbers:

1	ESTONIAN	5	MOLDAVIAN
2	LATVIAN	6	GEORGIAN
3	LITHUANIAN	7	ARMENIAN
4	BELORUSSIAN	8	AZERBAIDZHAN

0 100 200   400   600   800   1000

MILES

● UNION REPUBLIC CAPITALS

---- UNION REPUBLIC BOUNDARIES

1 Introduction

On 25 December 1991 Mikhail Sergeevich Gorbachev resigned as President of the Union of Soviet Socialist Republics (USSR), or Soviet Union. Six days later, at midnight, the Soviet Union itself was formally dissolved, and in its place 15 separate, independent states were formed. As late as August 1991, such an outcome had not been widely predicted, and it was certainly far from anybody's mind seven years previously. The fall of Soviet communism had implications reaching far beyond the fate of the world's largest country and its inhabitants. It spelt an end to the Cold War, which had dominated international politics for almost half a century, which had been fought out in 'Hot' form on the soil of Africa and southern and eastern Asia, and which threatened the world with the possibility of nuclear destruction. It dealt a severe and lasting blow to an ideology which had promised so much to ordinary people, particularly those suffering from poverty and injustice throughout the world, but which had delivered so little. So momentous was the shift that for a while all the talk was about a 'New World Order' or 'The End of History', until new and less readily identifiable enemies appeared. Above all, it meant a dramatic change in the day-to-day lives of millions of Russians, Ukrainians, Lithuanians, Latvians, Estonians, Moldavians, Belarusans, Azeris, Georgians, Armenians, Kazakhs, Kirghiz, Uzbeks, Tadzhiks, Turkmeni and dozens of other smaller nationalities. And it all seemed to have happened so easily: a man called Mikhail Gorbachev became leader of the Soviet Union and made some changes, things got out of hand, and the whole thing collapsed. Only large-scale bloodshed in some of the southern republics cast a shadow over what was otherwise a largely peaceful demise. In Russia itself, which contained half the population of the Soviet Union, the violent loss of only three lives can be

1

directly attributed to the process of dismantling one of the most powerful states the world had ever seen.

In the years that followed, political scientists sought to explain what had happened, and what most of them had failed to foresee. Historians are, thankfully, less open to criticism on this score. But it is certainly incumbent on them to explain the past, and given the luxury of time and a more distant perspective, together with a growing pool of sources, they should be able to do so more thoroughly than their political science colleagues were able to in the immediate aftermath. Thirteen years on, at the time of writing, this process of explanation is only just beginning. The most comprehensive and thoughtful account of this period to date is by a political scientist, Jerry Hough's *Democratization and Revolution in the USSR, 1985–1991* [41]. But historical approaches remain relatively limited. Archival materials from the last years of the Soviet Union are either still classified or remain unused. Oral histories, which could be available, have not been collected in a systematic way. Those historians who do write about these events rely very much on journalistic accounts, memoirs and earlier works by political scientists and others. Very few have sought to conduct original research on the period. Most existing historical accounts are included as part of broader histories of the Soviet Union, such as Robert Service's *A History of Twentieth Century Russia* [11] and Ronald Suny's *The Soviet Experiment* [12]. Biographies of Gorbachev provide more focus on this period and some, notably those by Archie Brown [54] and Martin McCauley [56], range much further than the main subject of their work. A shorter biographical work, by the Russian scholar Dmitri Volkogonov [13], did make use of archival material and provides quite different perspectives. Only a handful of full-length scholarly historical treatments focused on the subject – for example, Robert Strayer's *Why did the Soviet Union Collapse?* [5] and Edward Walker's *Dissolution* [43] have been written, though several attempts, such as Robert V. Daniels's *The End of the Communist Revolution* [2], treat the topic within a much broader historical and international perspective. Scholars of nationalism and of economics have taken a great interest in the final years of the Soviet Union, and it is their works and those of political scientists that continue to set the tone for understandings of the process as historians begin to make their way into the period. Consequently, the opinions and interpretations surveyed in this book are taken from a range of disciplines. The emphasis is on the relatively few historical treatments. On the whole, books written before 1991, though of great value at the time and not without insights today, are ignored for the purposes of this account since they lack the necessary historical perspective.

A further limitation of this survey is that it is restricted to works available in the English language. One of the positive consequences of the collapse of Communism from the point of view of Western scholars is that regular contact and the exchange of ideas between East and West became possible on a scale unimaginable only a few years earlier. Old habits die hard, however, and examples of direct collaboration, such as that between the economists Michael Ellman and Vladimir Kontorovich [71] are the exception rather than the rule. Among the negative consequences of the Soviet collapse have been a drastic reduction in funding available to academics and an ideological and methodological disorientation which have deterred Russian scholars from giving extensive treatment to this period, limiting the number of relevant works which have appeared. While Russian and other scholars have contributed different and valuable perspectives on the last years of the Soviet Union, as yet their works have not been incorporated into the dialogue of debate which is only just beginning to develop in Western countries, and their inclusion is beyond the scope of a work aimed at introducing Western students to these discussions.

As a result of the small number of historical treatments and the chronological proximity of these events, no clear schools of historical interpretation have emerged analogous to the totalitarian/revisionist controversy over the nature of the Soviet Union under Stalin. A number of different answers have been offered, however, to the fundamental question, why did Communism collapse in the Soviet Union? It is important to note here that expressions such as 'Soviet collapse' might refer to either or both of two processes which, while clearly linked, can be treated distinctly: one is the end of a system of state rule which had been initiated by the revolution of 1917 and whose most important characteristics, at least since Stalin's time, were the monopoly of politics by a single party, the Communist Party of the Soviet Union; the centrally planned economy; the hegemony of an official 'Marxist–Leninist' ideology; and the absence in reality of democracy and broader political and individual rights. The second process was the disintegration of the

USSR, which had been constructed as a federation of national republics in 1923, into 15 completely independent states in 1991. This book covers both processes, as do most existing works on the period. Indeed the extent to which these two processes can be treated as distinct, or else inevitably linked to each other, is one of the areas of controversy.

The clearest way in which treatments of the fall of Soviet communism are divided is over the length of perspective that is applied. Many adopt the long-term view that the Soviet system, while successful in transforming the former Russian Empire into a powerful industrial state, contained within itself the seeds of its own destruction. Systemic weaknesses, a redundant ideology, internal contradictions, and the absence of the flexibility required to adapt to changing environments and challenges meant that, even if its collapse need not have occurred exactly when and in the way it did, it was ultimately inevitable. Alternatively, it is possible to focus on the last few years of the Soviet Union and look at particular contingent factors, unexpected events and coincidences and, above all, the policy path pursued by Gorbachev, as explanatory factors in describing the fall. Linked to these two perspectives are disagreements as to whether the collapse of the communist order in the Soviet Union was, indeed, inevitable [5: 7–20]. A number of recent works explore the longer term perspective [2, 4, 6]. The approach taken by this book is very much focused on the events of 1985–91. In exploring the actual events that led up to the fall of Soviet communism, some light can be shed on whether these immediate causes were themselves contingent on contemporary events and circumstances, or were rather the product of longer term weaknesses.

Three main factors are seen as contributing to a greater or lesser extent to the collapse: the economy, Gorbachev's policies and nationalism. The bulk of this book is devoted to these themes, together with others which touch on one or more of the main themes, such as the international environment, social change and the role of Boris Yeltsin.

The first four chapters of the book provide only that background on the Soviet system which is essential to following the remainder of the account. The final chapter in Part One looks in more depth at one of the areas of controversy involved, namely the background, ideas and character of the two principal actors in the final drama of the Soviet Union, Mikhail Gorbachev and Boris Yeltsin.

Part Two concentrates on the years 1985–89 and examines the political and economic reforms of Gorbachev and the political environment in which he was operating. Part Three focuses more on the final two and a half years, and looks at the forces emerging from below – national movements, workers' and other forms of mass protest, and the regime's response, before covering the specific events that culminated in the fall of Soviet communism. While the book is organised thematically, it also follows a rough chronological structure.

Although the events discussed are historically recent they may not be remembered by the majority of today's students, and for an older generation, the memory can always use refreshing. Each chapter therefore includes a summary account of the events and developments under discussion, indicating controversies over particular points, before concluding with a general discussion of alternative interpretations. Existing scholarship presents a powerful case for providing prominence to each of these factors in the Soviet collapse. It is the present author's view that it was the unique combination of a number of these factors, both long-term and short-term, which led to the demise of Soviet communism in the manner and at the time that it did. The Conclusion argues that the state of historical research has not progressed to the stage where we can be more precise about which factors were more important than others, or even reach a definitive conclusion as to whether the collapse was inevitable or not. Consequently, differences in emphasis and interpretation are recorded impartially, and the reader is left to form his or her own opinion (with the aid of a guide to further reading) as to how the world changed at the end of 1991, and why it changed in the way it did.

Part One: Background

2 The Soviet Political System

While it had its roots in the Bolshevik Revolution of October 1917, the Soviet political system developed into a form which retained some of its essential features until the very end under the leadership of Iosif Stalin in the 1930s. In the early years of the Cold War, historical treatments of the Stalinist system were dominated by the totalitarian model. This model posited a society which was rigidly controlled from the top-down, in which no area of life was autonomous, and in which a single ideology dominated not only politics, but culture, leisure and ideas in general. This model was later challenged by revisionist historians who looked at social forces and competing interests at the higher levels of politics as defining the system, which also provided the potential for radical change. Since the opening of the Soviet archives to scholars in the late 1980s, a wealth of studies which adhered to neither school revealed a degree of complexity and differentiation which even the revisionists had not envisaged [16].

The arguments between historians taking these different approaches were often fractious or personal. They disagreed on the origins of the system, its governing forces and potential for variation. Many of the system's essential features were obvious and uncontested. Communism as it developed in the Soviet Union was strictly authoritarian. Elections were a sham, with citizens forced to vote for a single approved candidate. The state was backed up by an extensive secret police and a repressive system which reached its height during Stalin's Great Terror of 1937–38, but which thereafter continued to clamp down on any form of dissent. The press, television and radio were strictly controlled by the state, and freedom of expression was absent even in private settings.

Formally, the country was governed through a system of soviets, or councils. A regular political system of ministries with responsibility for different areas of policy was topped by a Council of Ministers and Prime Minister. But real power lay in the hands of the Communist Party of the Soviet Union (CPSU). The CPSU controlled appointments at all levels, and individuals usually rose up through the political system at the same time as climbing through the ranks of the Party. Appointments and promotions were controlled through a system known as the *nomenklatura* – a list of names, from which appointees could be chosen by their superiors. The CPSU was the only legal party, and its leading role was enshrined in the constitution. At the head of the CPSU was its Central Committee (CC) made up largely of the secretaries of Party organisations at the provincial and local level together with members of the government based in Moscow. But the CC met irregularly, and for most of its history never did more than rubber stamp decisions that were put to it on a strictly controlled agenda. Attached to the CC was its Secretariat, a body which wielded considerable influence through its role in making appointments. Ultimate authority was wielded by the CC's Political Bureau – the Politburo – numbering usually no more than ten members who met regularly. The senior figure in the Politburo was the General Secretary of the CPSU – Iosif Stalin from 1922 to 1953, Nikita Khrushchev from 1953 to 1964, Leonid Brezhnev from 1964 to 1982, Yuri Andropov from 1982 to 1984, Konstantin Chernenko from 1984 to 1985 and Mikhail Gorbachev from 1985 to 1991. When one General Secretary died, his successor was chosen by existing Politburo members. Although the Politburo was to some extent a collective body, its General Secretary's authority was hardly ever challenged. Almost all members of the Politburo, and a vast majority of Central Committee members, were men [19].

This political system changed little between 1934 and 1985. It was subjected to a number of shocks, most notably the external shock of the Second World War, or Great Patriotic War as it was known in the Soviet Union. There were further shocks under

Khrushchev, who tried to shake up the system during his rule by reorganising ministries, decentralising some areas of decision-making, and even dividing the Party into separate industrial and agricultural branches. When a conspiracy of his Politburo colleagues backed up by a majority of the CC responded by removing him in 1964, this only seemed to confirm the inbuilt conservatism and resistance to change within the system. Under Brezhnev politics atrophied, with the average age of Politburo members topping 70 and the loyalty of the rest of the Party assured by more or less guaranteeing jobs for life.

In these circumstances, there appeared little prospect of the political system reforming either itself or other areas of society. The appearance as General Secretary of the relatively young Mikhail Gorbachev in 1985 did not seem to break the pattern, as he had himself risen through this system in the regular way. The changes that ensued were therefore a shock to Western observers, but probably a much greater shock to the loyal servants of the regime.

Underpinning the political system was the official ideology of Marxism–Leninism which, while based on the writings of the two great founders of communism and retaining certain key features over time, was flexible enough to adapt to changing circumstances and the priorities of particular leaders. This ideology portrayed the Soviet Union as the vanguard proletarian state, which was moving inexorably towards the abolition of class differences and was inherently superior to capitalism in both its economic potential and the possibilities it provided for human development. It also justified the unchallenged leading role of the CPSU. A tight system of censorship and state control of the media, education and the arts backed up the ideology, so that it came to permeate most areas of life and its slogans were constantly proclaimed to the population in posters, radio broadcasts, schoolroom and university instruction, cinemas and theatres. Official prescriptions dulled creative ability and led to the promotion of mediocrity in culture, though imaginative intellectuals like the film-maker Tarkovsky were able to get around the censors and put across subtle messages, and others like Boris Pasternak and Alexander Solzhenitsyn could take advantage of occasional thaws to get their unorthodox works published. But the overall impact of the constant stream of formulaic phrases, coupled with the fact that they were so obviously in conflict with the realities of life in the Soviet Union, rendered the ideology more and more empty and meaningless as time went on. It seems that the majority of Soviet citizens grew to accept this, and simply ignored or dismissed the propaganda, substituting a corpus of verbally circulated jokes and pithy sayings, like 'they pretend to pay us, and we pretend to work'. Importantly, however, the system of ideology and censorship denied the population the possibility of access to alternative ideas and knowledge of what was happening in the West up until the Gorbachev period. Instances of social unrest were almost unheard of after the 1920s, and when they did occur, were rapidly met with either repression or concession so that news of their happening would only spread to other parts of the country by word of mouth and well after they had been dealt with. In these circumstances it was left to a small but dedicated, brave and effective band of dissidents, who first emerged in the wake of Khrushchev's secret speech denouncing Stalin in 1956, to maintain any semblance of opposition to Soviet ideology and policies.

One part of the official ideology was the commitment to spreading the revolution across the rest of the industrialised world and, later, the developing world. After 1923, this did not amount to much in practice, as the Soviet state was too weak in the 1920s, and in the 1930s Soviet diplomacy was engaged in the development of a series of pragmatic alliances needed to ensure survival as the threat of war loomed. In the Great Patriotic War of 1941–45 the Soviet Union not only defeated Hitler's armies but emerged as a genuine world Superpower. Between 1945 and 1949, Moscow was able to impose communist regimes on the countries of Eastern Europe which fell within its 'sphere of influence', building up a network of client states that were largely subordinated to Soviet military and economic interests.

But communism was not so readily accepted in the countries of Central and Eastern Europe which had enjoyed independence and at least limited forms of democracy between the wars, as well as having histories, cultures and broad institutions like the Catholic Church in Poland, all of which tended to reinforce opposition. Citizens of these countries, particularly East Germany, were less cut off from Western Europe through the ability to pick up radio broadcasts and greater opportunities for travel. In Poland in 1956, 1970 and 1980–81, Hungary in 1956 and Czechoslovakia in 1968, movements developed which threatened head-on the Moscow imposed communist orthodoxies. In Hungary and Czechoslovakia, military action was taken on Moscow's orders in order to put the movements down. While repression and, at times, flexibility succeeded in keeping the satellite states in line until 1989, the maintenance of a Soviet sphere of influence clearly carried risks as well as advantages. Even without these disturbances, within the broader communist bloc the Soviet Union faced tensions and challenges to her hegemony, from Yugoslavia and China in particular, both of which promoted alternative models of communism and refused to bow to Moscow's leadership.

The Soviet Union often pursued its own foreign policy interests through the network of Communist Parties and affiliates that had spread across both the industrialised and developing world by the time of the Second World War. These parties often enjoyed mass support and even entered into government on occasion, but their influence waned in the later Soviet period, and especially after the events in Czechoslovakia in 1968 led to widespread disillusionment among foreign supporters of the Soviet system.

The imposition of communism in Eastern Europe combined with other factors to create the Cold War between the Soviet Union and the USA. The development of nuclear weapons ensured that both sides devoted considerable effort to matching and, if possible, surpassing each other's nuclear arsenals. But given the relative sizes of the two economies the burden of defence spending was uneven, with the Soviet Union spending, at a conservative estimate, 15 per cent of the state budget on the military and possibly as much as 25 per cent. This commitment severely restricted the room for improvement in other areas of the economy. The Cold War came close to direct military action between the two superpowers over Cuba, Korea and Vietnam, but was mostly fought out in different ways, through lending support to different sides in internal conflicts in Africa and Asia, as well as in stockpiling weapons of mass destruction. After a thaw in relations in the 1970s, Ronald Reagan's presidency in the USA initially lent new impetus to the Cold War, and tensions increased following the shooting down of a Korean civilian airliner which had wandered into Soviet airspace in 1983. The latest Soviet adventure into the developing world, the invasion of Afghanistan in 1979, brought humiliation and demoralisation to the mighty Soviet Red Army, piling further pressure on Brezhnev's successors to adopt a new approach to international policy [37, 2: *136–62*].

Many histories of the Khrushchev and Brezhnev periods are dominated by the international situation, a fact which testifies in equal measure to global tensions and to domestic Soviet stability. But the very emphasis on stability since 1964 was one of the roots of future problems. As long as domestic tranquillity prevailed, the political system itself appeared to be effective. But political stagnation promoted both complacency and inflexibility, so that when a need for change did arise, as the result of either external or internal pressures, politics would inevitably be slow to respond and would prove a brake on reform.

3 The Soviet Economy

The economic system which was to fail so drastically in the late 1980s was based on the centrally planned economy, known sometimes as the command economy. All factories and farms belonged to the state, and economic activity was governed from above. A series of planning agencies, the chief of which was the State Planning Commission, *gosplan*, set production targets for each section of industry or agriculture, while at lower levels individual targets were set for factories and farms. Prices of consumer goods were also set by the planning agencies and the movement of materials and goods between enterprises were all subject to planning rather than buying and selling. Agriculture was organised into collective farms, *kolkhozy* and state farms, *sovkhozy*, which operated along much the same lines as industrial enterprises, although *kolkhozy* were allowed to make some profit from produce which exceeded the set targets and could be sold on the market. Employment and wages were also subjected to state control.

From 1928 this system was governed by a series of five-year plans which set the overall growth targets for the period. Almost invariably, the production actually achieved fell short of the plan targets. All the same, in the 1930s the economy achieved spectacular growth rates, transforming the Soviet Union from a relatively backward rural country into an industrial power which was capable of resisting Hitler's armies and eventually became one of the world's two superpowers. Officially, the Soviet economy grew at a rate of 13.9 per cent per year in the 1930s, although later estimates put the true figure as low as 3.2 per cent per year [23]. Although the Soviet Union never caught up with the USA in the size of its economy, there were times, most notably in the 1950s, when it appeared (misleadingly, as it turned out) to be moving ahead in the development of the latest technologies involved in nuclear missiles and the Space Race.

But even in the early years of high growth, weaknesses in the system were evident. In addition to the obvious human cost and suffering involved in industrialisation, it was clear that a tremendous amount of output was being lost as waste. It was also soon apparent that while the economy could be forced to expand by building new industries, exploiting the country's vast raw materials reserves and transferring people from the countryside to the cities, there was relatively little improvement over time in the amount of industrial output per worker employed (productivity). As time passed and the growth of the workforce slowed, so did the rate of economic growth. By 1973–74, the Soviet economy had entered a marked slowdown [24], and by the 1980s the economy had almost ceased to grow altogether.

There were a number of reasons for this. The absence of market forces and a low priority for the production of consumer goods meant that there was little incentive for workers to work hard or to seek to improve their position. Plan targets were set unrealistically high, and once one sector of the economy failed to meet its targets, other sectors which depended on its output were unable to continue production beyond a certain point, since they lacked the mechanism to transfer between workers or sectors the machinery left idle. Transport was chaotic, leading to further delays and waste when essential materials did not arrive. The immediate imperative to meet plan targets meant that little attention was paid to replacing or maintaining outdated or ageing machinery, and therefore machines were often in use for many years past their intended lifetime. This was one of the factors contributing to a high number of breakdowns and industrial accidents. The same imperative induced factory directors and farm managers to engage in deception. The trick was to get your plan targets set as low as possible so that it would be easier to surpass them and reap the bonuses awarded for doing so. This encouraged misinformation and corruption which became a regular feature of the planning process. And if a factory failed to fulfil its targets, the director could always lie, or blame someone else. The overall result was that the planners may have had a highly distorted view of the economy they were directing. Where shortages occurred, they could only be overcome by using influence or straightforward bribery with superiors or other enterprises. The CPSU was entwined with the production process as much as it was with politics, so much so that planning and production became largely a matter of politics as well as of economics. This made reform difficult, since the CPSU secretaries who were responsible for transmitting orders from the centre were often closely allied with local enterprise directors and managers, if they were not actually the same person.

These and other factors explain why the economic system was wasteful and inefficient at all times, but not why it slowed down so much in the 1980s. The slowdown might have been more marked earlier had it not been for the 1970s rise in oil prices, as the Soviet Union was a major exporter of oil. In addition to the long-term problem of replacing 'extensive' with 'intensive' growth, the political and social stagnation of the Brezhnev years does seem to have made the situation worse. Workers and managers alike, secure in their posts provided they did not step out of line, became complacent about the need to improve output. A further factor was the growing pressure to match the USA in terms of armaments production, while the maintenance of the Soviet empire in Eastern Europe may actually have been a drain on the economy [21, 22, 25].

4 The Nationalities Question

A major feature of the Soviet Union was its multinational nature and state structure. In 1926, ethnic Russians made up only 47 per cent of the total population of the USSR, rising to 50.8 per cent in 1989. The next largest national group in 1989 was the Ukrainians, at 15.5 per cent. Then came Uzbeks (5.8 per cent), Belorussians (3.5 per cent), Kazakhs (2.8 per cent) and Tatars (2.3 per cent). The other nationals who had their 'own' republics in 1991 – Armenians, Tadzhiks, Azeris, Latvians, Georgians, Moldavians, Lithuanians, Turkmen, Kyrgyz and Estonians, each constituted less than 2 per cent of the total population. A further 69 nationalities were officially recognised on Soviet territory, meaning that the Soviet Union was a genuinely multinational state consisting of one major group (Russians) and numerous smaller ones.

After the Russian Revolution of 1917, most of the larger nationalities of the Russian Empire were governed for a time by their own independent national governments during the period of Civil War. Poland, Finland, Estonia, Latvia and Lithuania, retained their independence. All the others were replaced by local Soviet governments, often following the intervention of the Red Army, by early 1921. Estonia, Latvia and Lithuania, after twenty years of independence, were reincorporated during the course of the Second World War, together with a part of eastern Romania which became the Moldavian Republic. The Bolsheviks had promised the right of self-determination to these peoples, but looked for ways to integrate them into the Soviet framework. The solution adopted in 1923 was to create a federal system, the USSR. This consisted initially of three republics plus the Transcaucasian Federation.

The division of the Transcaucasian Federation into three republics, and of Central Asia into five, plus the addition of new territories during the Second World War, brought the total number of Union Republics up to 15 after 1945. Although varying greatly in size of territory and population, they each had, in theory, an equal status in the federal system and were supposed to enjoy self-government in areas like education, justice and culture. With one exception, they each had their own branch of the CPSU, their own ministries mirroring the ministries of the Soviet Union in Moscow and, for most of the time, their own official language alongside Russian as the *lingua franca* of the whole Soviet Union.

The exception was the largest republic – The Russian Soviet Federative Socialist Republic, or RSFSR. It made up about three quarters of the territory and contained over half of the Soviet Union's population. As its title suggests, it was itself a federation within a federation, containing 17 Autonomous Republics (as opposed to the more powerful Union Republics) and numerous smaller national territories. In all, non-Russian national minorities made up 18.5 per cent of the RSFSR population in 1989. Moscow was the capital of both the RSFSR and the USSR, and the USSR ministries governed the RSFSR without having to operate through the intermediate ministries that operated in other Republics. Much the same was the case with the Communist Party. That changed during the final years of the Soviet Union, when the perception that Russians were discriminated against by not being allowed their own institutions had become a cause of complaint and basis for political mobilisation. On the other hand, it has to be pointed out that ethnic Russians dominated the higher levels of both the state and the CPSU, while the Russian language and culture took prime place across the USSR.

Among the other republics histories, cultures and traditions of nationalism varied enormously. Geographically, they can be divided into four groups: the Baltic republics of Estonia, Latvia, and Lithuania; the western republics of Ukraine, Belorussia (now Belarus) and Moldavia (now Moldova); the Transcaucasian republics of Georgia, Azerbaijan and Armenia; and the Central Asian Republics of Kazakhstan, Uzbekistan, Kyrgyzstan, Tadzhikistan and Turkmenistan. The Belorussians and Ukrainians were Slavs – that is to say, their languages and cultures were related to those of the Russians. Most of the population of Azerbaijan and the five Central Asian republics were Muslim, and were ethnically closer to the Turkic or Persian peoples than to the Europeans. Before 1917, there was little conception of national identity in Central Asia, where people were more likely to identify with their clans or religions, and where numerous different, but related, languages were spoken. At the other extreme, the Georgians had a long tradition of nationhood and a strong sense of national identity. The Lithuanians, Latvians and Estonians developed a stronger sense of national identity as a result of their 20 years of independence. Among the smaller nations, the Chechens of the North Caucasus region of the RSFSR were notable for their fierce sense of national pride and had a history of resistance to Russian and Soviet rule, while the Tatars formed a powerful national group in the middle of the RSFSR.

Another variation between the national republics was the proportion of the population which belonged to the 'titular' nationality. In 1989 Armenians were 93.3 per cent of the population of the Armenian Soviet Socialist Republic (SSR), but Latvians and Kirgiz made up a bare majority in their republics while Kazakhs were only 39.7 per cent of the population of the Kazakh SSR and were almost outnumbered by Russians. From the 1930s onwards, there was a steady flow of Russians, and to some extent Ukrainians, into the other republics, and their presence was a particular source of resentment in the Estonian and Latvian SSRs.

To a limited extent these differences were levelled out by Soviet policies. In the 1920s languages were standardised and national symbols and works of culture were created for those national territories which did not have them. In the 1930s the Russian language and culture were promoted more vigorously and increasingly stood for the whole of the Soviet Union. During the war, a number of national groups, such as the Chechens and the Tatars of the Crimea, were forcibly deported from their homelands and resettled in scattered groups in Kazakhstan and Siberia.

The official ideology of Marxism–Leninism was in theory at odds with national sentiment. For most of the Soviet period, manifestations of nationalism were met with persecution or demotion, but in the Brezhnev period in particular, republican leaders served for a long time and were able to establish their own power bases and to promote national causes within certain limits. Historians are divided as to whether the purpose of Soviet nationality policies was

18

to Russify the whole population, promote a single Soviet identity, or to maintain separate identities within a federal system and under the unifying control of the CPSU. In any case, while most people spoke Russian at least as a second language, and often as a first language, national differences, in part maintained by the federal system and the actions of republican leaders, never looked like disappearing.

For most of the Soviet period, open expressions of national discontent were sporadic, but not unknown. Demonstrations around national demands in Georgia, Kazakhstan, Ingushetia and Abkhazia in the 1960s and 1970s were, on a small scale, previews of the events of the late 1980s. On a day-to-day level national tensions could be observed in a number of situations – sporting events, mixed schools, or between individuals standing in queues – but these rarely erupted into open violence [29: 68–71]. There are clear indications that, at times, either local republican leaders or the central authorities were inclined to encourage these tensions in at least a mild form, perhaps as a form of divide and rule or to distract the people from the manifest failings of the communist system, and in order to provide the regime with an alternative source of legitimacy [34: 121–4].

There had been a history of ethnic conflict, particularly during the civil war years of 1918–20, and earlier under the Russian Empire. The most violent conflicts were between Armenians and Muslim Azeris, who competed for jobs and influence in cities like Baku and who contested the territory of Nagorno–Karabakh. Although these conflicts disappeared for most of the Soviet period, they were to re-emerge in an even bloodier form at the end of the 1980s.

Inasmuch as there were reasons for nationalities to engage in rivalry with each other or to resent Russian-dominated Soviet rule, a number of factors kept these in check: repression directed against nationalism, an ideology and education system aimed at promoting the 'brotherhood of nations', an economic system which, while failing to promote affluence, delivered a certain level of comfort and job security from the 1960s onwards and the latitude allowed to the national republics in certain spheres. The removal of some or all of these factors under Gorbachev's *glasnost* were at least to some extent responsible for the emergence of national movements which played such a prominent role in the fall of Soviet communism [30, 31, 33].

5 Early Attempts at Reform

The problems with the economy which were evident from the first years of the planning system led to a number of attempts to reform it. In the 1930s the Stakhanovite movement, which rewarded individual workers for performing feats of high production, sought to encourage the workforce as a whole to work harder. Other campaigns and disciplinary measures were aimed at the same end of increasing productivity. In the 1950s and early 1960s, Nikita Khrushchev tackled the system itself, trying to devolve a certain amount of decision-making to the local level and reorganising the Party and the central ministries. The backlash against these measures, which led to Khrushchev's downfall, showed how the vested interests of local officials, enterprise directors and even workers, militated against any thoroughgoing reform. Half-hearted attempts in the early Brezhnev years, aimed at introducing incentives for higher production by allowing enterprises to dispose of their own excess profits, were quickly abandoned in the face of apathy. No further significant attempts at reforming either the political or the economic system were made until the 1980s.

Before Gorbachev, the Soviet leader who seemed most likely to pursue a consistent reform programme was Yuri Andropov, who succeeded Brezhnev as General Secretary in November 1982 until his own death in February 1984. From his former position as head of the KGB, Andropov was already better informed than his Politburo colleagues of the real state of Soviet society, and the declining rates of economic growth and rising discontent were giving cause for alarm. Andropov's initial concern was to tackle lack of discipline in the workplace and corruption in the state and Party. In the process, he upset the 'stability of cadres', which had characterised the Brezhnev period, by dismissing some 20 per cent of ministers and regional Party secretaries in just over a year. Whether this initial drive, which was similar to the early months of Gorbachev's office, might have developed into a more far-reaching reform programme is a debatable point. In any case, his death after a little more than a year in office proved to be an initial relief to the grandees of Soviet politics, who chose the safe and uninspiring Konstantin Chernenko as his successor.

Each of these reform programmes suffered similar fates. Efforts to improve productivity and discipline had little impact as workers were rarely offered real incentives and found ways to get around new restrictions. Systemic reforms which threatened to upset the comfortable position of enterprise directors and regional Party officials were invariably blocked if not openly opposed and had little real effect. If anything, such reforms increased the tendency of officials to provide misinformation and engage in further cooperation with each other against the reforming authorities. Collusion between workers and managers to ensure minimum disruption to the established routines of both was not an uncommon response. All this serves to underline the difficulties Mikhail Gorbachev would face when he chose to embark on his own programme of reform.

6 Gorbachev and Yeltsin

Two figures above all dominate the history of the final years of the Soviet system: Mikhail Sergeyevich Gorbachev and Boris Nikolaevich Yeltsin. Initially, the two were allies: Gorbachev brought Yeltsin to Moscow to lead the Construction Department of the CC in April 1985, and rapidly promoted him to the post of Secretary of the CC within three months, to head of the Moscow City Communist Party organisation (*Gorkom*) in December of the same year, and candidate (non-voting) membership of the Politburo of the CPSU. Although it was the conservative Yegor Ligachev who first pushed Yeltsin's promotion, impressed by the determination and organisational ability he had displayed as First Secretary of the Sverdlovsk regional party organisation, he soon became identified as the most radical reformer in the top Party leadership and a supporter of the more controversial aspects of Gorbachev's programme until his dismissal from the Moscow *Gorkom* in November 1987 and the Politburo in February 1988. After a time in the political wilderness, Yeltsin's return to a position of prominence as Chairman of the Supreme Soviet of the Russian republic in May 1990, and his popular election as Russia's president the following year, meant that the rivalry between the two men became the focus of politics in the final years and months of the Soviet Union.

The role that this personal rivalry may have played in the breakup of the Soviet Union is discussed again in Chapter 16. First it is necessary to discuss the question of personal motivation and belief which divides historical opinion over both men. Were either of them committed radical reformers from early on in their careers, as both were later to claim, or does the fact that both owed their advancement to loyal service at lower levels of the Communist

Party suggest that their initial motivation was to preserve the Soviet system? In Gorbachev's case, two of his British biographers, Archie Brown and Martin McCauley, ascribe great importance to his early experiences and suggest that he was a supporter of reform from a young age. Both of Gorbachev's grandfathers were victims of Stalin's terror in the 1930s – one for failing to fulfil the plan for crop sowing in 1933, and the other accused of activities in a Trotskyist organisation in 1937. While the former survived prison and exile, the latter was executed [54: 25–6, 56: 15–17]. The second formative experience was the effect of the Second World War on Gorbachev. When his father was called up to the army the young Mikhail was burdened with family responsibilities at the early age of 11. The occupation of his home village, Privolnoe, by the German army both presented an immediate danger to Gorbachev as the son of a communist, and threatened to pose an obstacle to his career after the war, when inhabitants of formerly occupied regions were generally treated as suspect by the Soviet regime. Personal experience of the horrors of war also left a deep mark on his character and world outlook [56: 17].

Gorbachev was active in Soviet politics in the late Stalin period, in the Komsomol (Communist Youth) organisation in Stavropol, and then as a student in the Law Faculty of Moscow University from 1950 to 1955, becoming a candidate member of the CPSU in 1951. At this time he came into contact with a number of intellectuals both among his peers and his lecturers who influenced his own thought, while his studies of Soviet law 'opened his eyes to some of the discrepancies between Soviet propaganda and real life' [54: 31]. Among his new acquaintances was a Czech communist, Zdenek Mlynář. Gorbachev kept up his friendship by correspondence with Mlynář, who was later involved in the Czech Communist reform movement culminating in the events of 1968 which became known as the Prague Spring. Gorbachev himself visited Prague in 1969, and later claimed that the resentment he felt among the Czech population to the Warsaw Pact's military intervention of the previous year left him feeling 'uncomfortable' [54: 41].

In 1955 Gorbachev turned his back on a career in law and directed his full attention to politics, returning to his native Stavropol region and rising by 1970 to the most powerful position in the region – First Secretary of the regional Party organisation, at the relatively young age of 39. Before and after this appointment he was deeply involved in agriculture, and marked himself out as a supporter of reforms which aimed to improve agricultural productivity by allowing more initiative for individual producers and collective farms in both their methods of farming and the disposal of their products. Central resistance to such measures provided, according to McCauley, an important lesson for the future leader: 'Gorbachev perceived this as a classic example of the Party apparatus protecting its privileges at the expense of economic efficiency. Had farms been permitted to use their initiative, Soviet agriculture would have produced much more food … and saved the country billions of dollars in imports' [56:27]. As regional party leader Gorbachev continued to concentrate on improving local agriculture, but by the more acceptable means of negotiating successfully for a greater share of central investment in local projects, such as the Stavropol canal which was completed in 1978, rather than by challenging orthodoxy by proposing unacceptable reforms. His biographers conclude that observing the rules of the game in this manner frustrated Gorbachev and led him to develop a more general critique of the Soviet system, which he thought stifled initiative from below and made it 'actually impossible to do something worthwhile if one observed all the rules and regulations' [56: 34].

Nevertheless, Gorbachev achieved sufficient successes at the local level while staying within the bounds of Party norms to attract the attention of powerful figures in Moscow, most notably KGB head and Brezhnev's future successor Yuri Andropov, Politburo member Mikhail Suslov and Prime Minister Aleksei Kosygin. In November 1978, Gorbachev was brought to Moscow as Central Committee Secretary for Agriculture. In this capacity he was able to experience at first hand the inertia of the ageing leaders under Brezhnev, but openly backed the leadership, including over the controversial invasion of Afghanistan, realising that any hope he had of further political progress rested on maintaining solidarity with the Politburo (which he joined in 1979). He was able to introduce minor but significant changes in agriculture, such as the abolition of payments to tractor drivers on the basis of the number of hectares they ploughed, and he consulted more widely with specialists than was the common practice among leading politicians [54: 55–60]. Even after Brezhnev's death and in the more reformist climate of the Andropov leadership, Gorbachev soon found that there were limits to how far reform could be pushed, and recognised that

Kremlin politics would make it inadvisable for him to make a direct bid for power against the older generation after Andropov's death in February 1984. His accession to the top post after Chernenko's death only 13 months later owed much to his success in remaining apart from the political intrigues of other Politburo members.

But he would still not have become General Secretary at this time if the other leaders had been opposed to his policy stance, and there were already clear indications before Chernenko's death that Gorbachev was prepared to go further down the path of reform than had hitherto been contemplated. In a speech Gorbachev delivered to a meeting on ideology in December 1984, he used the terms *perestroika* (restructuring) and *uskorenie* (acceleration) in explaining the need for far-reaching reform of the economy, as well as referring to the need to introduce elements of democracy into the Soviet system. He also made a positive impression as someone who differed from the usual mould of the Soviet politician on a visit to Britain in the same month, when British Prime Minister Margaret Thatcher made her often quoted assessment 'I like Mr. Gorbachev. We can do business together' [54: *77–80*, 56: *44–51*].

For his biographers, then, Gorbachev had become deeply committed to reform and opposed to Stalinist excesses as a result of both his early personal experiences and his ability to witness first hand the inefficiency of the economy and the difficulties to be met in promoting change under the existing system. His failure to break ranks openly with communist orthodoxy at an earlier stage simply reflected his realisation that to do so would only lead to marginalisation, excluding him from any possibility of bringing about change from within as well as, perhaps, frustrating any personal ambition he nurtured.

But it should be remembered that it was only after a period of minor tinkering that Gorbachev moved gradually towards a more radical reform programme. Others have seen Gorbachev's development as a late reaction to otherwise insoluble problems rather than the product of any longstanding commitment to change. According to the Russian historian Dmitri Vologonov, Gorbachev had no intention of dismantling the system: 'He was the leader during the transition, the advocate of change as a process of the "perfection, improvement, acceleration, and finally the restructuring", or *perestroika*, of the Communist system' [13: *434*]. Volkogonov labels

Gorbachev as 'the last Leninist' who 'implemented Party directives expeditiously' [13: *440*]. Although he recognised more clearly than his colleagues the need for reform, and possessed certain personal qualities and the temperament of an innovative leader, he consistently justified his reforms in Leninist terms. This dogmatism hampered his programme, especially as it underlay his refusal to abandon his commitment to the exclusive role of the Communist Party. 'He still thought of restructuring it [the CPSU], when everyone else could see the futility of the task, as long as it clung to Leninist ideology' [13: *444–5*]. Historian Robert Service stands in between these positions, characterising Gorbachev as an enthusiastic Marxist–Leninist [11: *370*], who nevertheless was open to a range of ideas, was impressed by the economic achievements of capitalism and was deeply committed to achieving change [11: *437–8*].

To most contemporary observers, Gorbachev's new course and style of politics came as a big surprise that it was generally assumed that he, and later Yeltsin, represented an exceptional departure from the normal Soviet politician. This view was later maintained by Gorbachev's political biographers. Indeed, as we shall see, many explanations of the ultimate failure of Gorbachev's reform programme rest on the assumption that it was actively resisted by a majority of CPSU functionaries, particularly at the regional level. However, two important studies, by Jerry Hough and Wisła Suraska, challenge this widely accepted view. Instead, they propose that Gorbachev should be seen as representative of a much broader layer of politicians who were emerging into positions of importance in the early 1980s. Hough argues that the generation of communists below the Brezhnev generation, most of whose political careers belonged to the post-Stalin period, were of a different political outlook altogether and were growing impatient at the lack of change under the old leadership. This generation was firmly established in the regional Party apparatus by the time of Chernenko's death, and it was their pressure, expressed through their dominance of the Central Committee, which may have prevailed on the Politburo to appoint Gorbachev as General Secretary [41: *65–79*]. Further support for the idea that the CPSU was not overwhelmingly opposed to reform is provided by Igor Prostiakov's personal testimony that the Politburo had approved radical economic reform measures in April 1984, some 11 months before Chernenko's death [71: *100–05*]. Suraska goes further in pointing

26

not only to the common background of the first generation of politicians to grow up under Stalin, but also to the influence of Western social science approaches and social democratic ideas which were made available, albeit on a highly controlled basis, to a select number of them. In this Suraska also sees a fundamental weakness of Gorbachev and his most radical advisers, whose schooling in Stalinist orthodoxy and later limited exposure to alternative ideas led to a combination of ignorance even of the Russian past and misperception of global developments, which in turn contributed to the intellectual poverty of their approach, however laudable their intentions [42: *12–32*].

We return to this argument in Chapter 11, but here it must be remembered that Gorbachev always operated within certain institutional constraints, most importantly that of the CPSU. Although the power of the General Secretary over the Party was enormous, the experience of Nikita Khrushchev serves as a reminder that he could not ignore the inclinations of the Party membership altogether. In such a vast country and a system as bureaucratic as that of the Soviet Union, the General Secretary was bound to depend on the CPSU not just to prop up his position, but also to implement his policy directives. Regional party secretaries could act as a power unto themselves in the areas under their jurisdiction (though always under the constraint that they could easily be removed from their posts), and had a collective voice in the CC of the CPSU, which had the power to confirm appointments and policies. Throughout this period the CC majority remained loyal to Gorbachev, although by 1990 at least it was demonstrating its independence in regularly voting down Gorbachev-backed candidates to important party posts. It is quite possible, however, that CC members were capable of standing in solidarity with Gorbachev in Moscow while simultaneously undermining his policies in the regions. This is one of the controversies we return to later.

Gorbachev's eventual nemesis, Boris Yeltsin, is, if anything, an even more controversial figure. Hailed in the West as a democrat and the saviour of Russia for his role in defeating the attempted coup of August 1991, later judgements have been more influenced by his behaviour as the first President of the post-Communist Russian Federation from 1991–2000. His forceful suppression of parliamentary opposition in 1993, examples of incompetence and accusations of large-scale corruption and nepotism suggested the

27

inheritance of some of the worst features of Soviet political life, which became all the more dangerous when freed from the institutional and ideological restrictions within which communist leaders had had to work. The constitution he succeeded in getting approved by a national referendum in 1993 gave him greater powers than any other elected president in the world, leading to fears of abuse which were only heightened by increasingly frequent public displays of inebriation.

But is it fair to project Yeltsin's later attitudes back onto his behaviour in the last years of the Soviet Union? Yeltsin himself was careful to underline a lifelong commitment to justice, efficiency and democracy in the first of a series of autobiographical works. He also portrayed himself as a man of principle and one of life's chancers, whose ambition and drive were in no way dimmed by several close brushes with death [52]. From an early stage, he understood how to endear himself to the people over whom he exercised authority [11: *504*], and his successful demagogy helps to explain both his fall from grace in 1987 and his subsequent spectacular return.

Like Gorbachev, Yeltsin owed his position to loyal service to his political bosses while distinguishing himself by his efficiency at the local level and, ultimately, openness to new ideas. He worked his way up initially through the construction industry, switching to a political career (not an unusual step for a successful manager) in 1968. From 1976 to 1985, as head of the Party organisation of Sverdlovsk province (whose capital was Russia's fifth largest city and an important industrial centre), he managed to combine personal popularity with the administrative and personal skills needed to get things done under the Soviet system. The results attracted the attention of his superiors, and in particular Gorbachev. Volkogonov (whose admiration for Yeltsin should be treated with caution given that he worked for him in the last years of his life), credits him, unlike Gorbachev, with breaking with Leninism at an early stage [13: *503*]. Certainly there is less evidence in Yeltsin's case of any deep interest in political theory. His offer to resign from his posts in the Moscow organisation and the Politburo in September 1987 (see Chapter 11), in the face of constant harassment by some of his colleagues, appears to indicate a committed and principled stand in favour of reform. On the other hand, many aspects of his behaviour in both the Soviet and post-Soviet periods (see Chapter 16) suggest a keenly calculated opportunism fired by personal ambition as much as anything else, with little regard for the political consequences. For example, his encouragement in 1990 to the autonomous republics of the RSFSR to 'seize as much autonomy as you can' (see Chapter 12) was aimed at weakening Gorbachev's position, but had consequences for his own rule later, including the promotion and radicalisation of his future opponent, the Chechen leader Dzhokar Dudaev.

The whole question of the actual political beliefs and commitment of Gorbachev and Yeltsin is to some extent academic. What is almost certainly true of Gorbachev, as illustrated in the following chapters, is that he pursued his reform policies inconsistently and without full conviction. Whether this was because he himself was ideologically uncertain, or because he was a realist who tried to achieve the impossible task of placating both conservatives and radicals in an effort to keep his programme on track, makes little practical difference in the end. The question of how important individuals are when compared to broader historical forces has always been a matter for debate between historians. Numerous individuals influenced the particular course of events which eventually sealed the fate of the Soviet Union – dissidents like Andrei Sakharov, republican leaders, the plotters behind the August coup, striking miners and demonstrators – as did unforeseen events like the Chernobyl disaster, not to mention external events in the West and Eastern Europe.

There is a strong case for argument that at a time of radical change and uncertainty, the personal beliefs and convictions of individual leaders has a greater influence on events than at more stable times, when institutional checks and balances and social pressures exert more of a long-term effect. George Breslauer, who has been able to directly compare Gorbachev and Yeltsin as leaders from the perspective of the end of Yeltsin's presidency, concludes that whether they were in the ascendancy or when their powers were waning, both leaders were able to contribute substantially to developments according to their own personality and choices: 'During a leader's stage of ascendancy, he tends to have greater room for political maneuver and greater latitude to allow his personal preferences and predispositions to reshape his program. During the stage of decline, the leader is embattled but approaches this struggle from a position of ascendancy and relative strength … Personal factors loom large in determining the choices a leader makes for how to combat the decline in his authority' [55: 40]. Against this it needs to be considered that both were, in different ways, reacting to developments unpredictably unleashed by *perestroika*, and thus between them offered a choice of alternatives which was ultimately resolved in Yeltsin's favour by forces much broader than one man's personality. If one takes the view that the collapse of Communism was systemic and inevitable, then the role of these individuals was ultimately irrelevant. But as far as the precise course of events goes, there is no doubt that Mikhail Gorbachev and Boris Yeltsin, both forceful personalities who left a deep impression on all those who came into contact with them, loom far larger than any others in this period and have left a mark, for better or for worse, on the history of Soviet communism and, indeed, the world.

Part Two: Reform from Above

---

7 Personnel and Policies

Mikhail Gorbachev's first pronouncements as General Secretary of the CPSU gave little indication of the turmoil that was to come. At the meeting of the Politburo which affirmed his appointment on 11 March 1985, shortly after Chernenko's death he assured his colleagues that there was 'no need to change our policies' [44: *3*]. In his acceptance speech he praised his predecessors, Brezhnev, Andropov and Chernenko, and promised to continue their policies. In private, however, the day before his appointment he had confided to his wife Raisa that 'life demands action, and has done so for a long time. No, we can't go on living like this any more' [13: *445*]. At the next meeting of the CPSU CC in April, he argued for a 'qualitatively new state of society' which was to be achieved by modernisation and the development of Soviet democracy. Such phrases were commonplace from Party leaders and could usually be safely ignored, but there were indications that Gorbachev really meant to bring about change. At a meeting in Leningrad in May 1985, he announced that 'obviously, we all of us must undergo reconstruction, all of us … Everyone must adopt new approaches and understand that no other path is available to us' [11: *441*].

Gorbachev's priority was the economy. Since at least the early 1970s, real output in the Soviet economy had effectively been stagnating (see Chapter 3 and Table 8.1 later). But his initial approach was largely characteristic of earlier, ineffectual attempts at reform.

31

Decentralisation of decision-making, an emphasis on cost account-ing and a few reshuffles of personnel all amounted to not much more than an exhortation to increase efficiency and output within the existing system (illustrated, for example, by his comments to the CC on 11 June 1985). Calls for improvements in the quality of finished goods echoed similar statements which had been made with depressing regularity over the previous 30 years. There was, nevertheless, something distinctly different about his approach. A week after his accession, a series of articles in *Pravda* called for a campaign against corruption in the management of the economy. While this had little immediate effect, its full significance became apparent later as it developed into Gorbachev's key policy of *Glasnost.*

Most significantly, in his first few months of office, Gorbachev moved to rebuild the leadership of the country by clearing out the 'Old Guard' of ageing dignitaries closely associated with the Brezhnev era and replace them with a more reform-minded younger generation. At first he moved cautiously. On 23 April 1985 the head of the KGB Viktor Chebrikov and the CPSU secretaries Nikolai Ryzhkov and Yegor Ligachev were promoted to full mem-bership of the Politburo, and Defence Minister Sergei Sokolov was appointed candidate (non-voting) member. All four were already senior members of the Communist Party and already in line for promotion, and their elevation would raise few eyebrows. They were hardly radicals, but Ryzhkov and Ligachev were to play key roles as moderate supporters of reform over the next few years, while also ultimately exerting a conservative influence on Gorbachev's programme [54: *107*]. At the same time Ligachev was appointed a senior secretary and effectively the number two in the CPSU, while Ryzhkov became Chairman of the Council of Ministers (roughly equivalent to Prime Minister) in September.

A clearer sign of Gorbachev's intent came at the beginning of July, when his main rival for the post of General Secretary at the time of Chernenko's death, Grigorii Romanov, was forced to retire from the Politburo. Among the new appointees were men who were more clearly associated with radical reform: Eduard Shevardnadze, who became Foreign Minister and launched a new era in Soviet–Western relations; and Boris Yeltsin. Yeltsin and Lev Zaykov were also appointed to the influential CPSU Secretariat. Further retirements from and appointments to the Politburo were announced in

February 1986, and Gorbachev completed the shift in influence by promoting the relatively junior but radical and competent Alexander Yakovlev to candidate membership of the Politburo in January 1987. In June, Yakovlev rose to full membership of the Politburo, taking the place of Defence Minister Sokolov, who was made to pay for the failings of the military exposed by the Mathias Rust affair (see Chapter 10). The shift in the Secretariat of the CPSU was even more immediate and profound, with only two of the secretaries from the Brezhnev era surviving to the end of Gorbachev's first year in power. Further changes in September 1988 and September 1989 completed the renewal of the Party's leading personnel. By 1988, 66 per cent of the members of the Party's CC had been appointed in Gorbachev's time, and most remaining members of the 'old guard' were forced out in the following year [44: *19–22*].

While Gorbachev was able to retire a number of leading representatives of the Old Guard without resistance, a bigger problem was what was to be done with the longest serving and most senior member of the Politburo, the highly respected Foreign Minister Andrei Gromyko. Gromyko had nominated Gorbachev to the General Secretaryship, and his standing internationally as well as at home made straightforward dismissal politically impossible. The problem was solved by elevating Gromyko to the position of Chairman of the Presidium of the Supreme Soviet of the USSR in July 1985 – in theory, the most senior position in the country, but in practice a figurehead who had no real power, although Gromyko did retain his seat in the Politburo until September 1988.

Similar changes took place at lower levels. In Gorbachev's first year he replaced 24 of the 72 first secretaries in the RSFSR's provincial Party organisations, and 23 out of 78 in the other Republics. Four first secretaries of the fourteen non-Russian Republics were changed at the same time. A further 19 changes of provincial secretaries were made by 1988. About 1 in 5 officials in local Party organisations lost their jobs in the first year, while 39 out of 101 Soviet ministers lost their jobs, as did thousands of lower officials.

Several writers point out that it was not unusual in the USSR for a newly appointed General Secretary to extensively reshuffle leading personnel in order to remove potential rivals to his authority and to ensure loyalty and a core of like-minded supporters. However, on this occasion, several important departures from the usual pattern have been noted. First, the scale of turnover could only be compared with the totally different circumstances of the years of Stalin's Great Terror. The speed of change was also unprecedented [41: *63–4*]. Then there was the nature of the new appointees. Unlike his predecessors, Gorbachev did not bring to Moscow people who had served under him in his old regional power base in Stavropol, preferring instead people whose abilities he had observed in Moscow [11: *459*]. Replacements in the senior positions were considerably younger than their predecessors – again, generational renewal was not uncommon in association with a change of leadership [17], but here the effect was greatly exaggerated. By the end of 1985, the average age of the Politburo members was 64, compared with 71 in 1982. By 1990 it had fallen to 55. The newly promoted officials were also generally much better educated than their predecessors [44: *22*].

Thus the personnel changes 'testify to the consensus at the top that the Brezhnev generation had to be swept away' [56: *54*]. But did this mean that Gorbachev now headed a reformist leadership? The next two most important people in the country, Ligachev and Ryzhkov, were, at best, moderate reformers, and as reform became more radical Ligachev would prove to be firmly in the conservative camp. One of Gorbachev's most trusted allies, Valery Boldin, turned out to be a powerful weapon for the conservatives. Boldin had been an aide of Gorbachev's since 1981, and was promoted to head the General Department of the CC in 1987, and to Chief of Staff in 1990. In both these positions, Boldin had considerable control over the papers and other sources of information which reached Gorbachev's desk, and invariably used his position to skew information in a conservative direction [54: *102*]. Brown argues that the appointment of Boldin was simply a mistake. But his was not an isolated case, and if Gorbachev's intention had been to create a reformist leadership, then his failure to do so more thoroughly needs some explaining. As we shall see, one of the possible factors inhibiting Gorbachev's reform programme was the need to keep people like Ligachev on his side. So why were they there at all?

To a large extent the answer to this question revolves around our understanding of the extent to which Gorbachev himself was clearly committed to a reform programme from the beginning, which has already been discussed (Chapter 6). In any case, if Gorbachev had wanted to promote reformers, there was a limited pool to choose from within the existing apparatus. McCauley suggests that the new generation 'had been groomed in the same political stable' as their predecessors [56: 54]. The new appointees were selected for their energy and qualifications rather than radical credentials – even Boris Yeltsin was at this point known only as an effective and popular regional leader rather than for any of his particular political or economic views [13: 498–9]. Given the large numbers of new personnel, Gorbachev would have been pressed to find committed reformers in sufficient numbers. Thus his appointments, especially at the middle and lower levels, were made on meritocratic rather than political grounds. But education and talent were no guarantee of support for reform, and without firm views there was always the risk that they would be swamped by their environment of bureaucracy and conservatism. Service argues that there was little choice in the selection of new cadres, since reliable and radical reformers like Yeltsin were appointed rarities. Consequently Gorbachev had to rely on people he had spotted in Moscow who, once they were appointed to responsible positions in the regions, 'went native' and quickly adapted to the prevalent old practices and attitudes [11: 449, 459]. The Communist Party, with its ideology, personal patronage and deeply ingrained inertia, had been the only school for developing political cadres. A further problem was that, in clearing out the old wood, Gorbachev also lost years of experience to be replaced by relatively raw talent. And very few of his appointees had any experience or understanding of the ways in which western societies and economies, which were eventually to provide the model for reform, worked [56: 55, 42: 26–8]. At a more fundamental level, if Gorbachev was to work through the Communist Party, he could not afford to alienate it. Most of its 19 million members had at least some reason to be fearful of any change which might threaten their way of life and, in at least some cases, deeply held political convictions [12: 452].

Some qualifications need to be reserved, then, over the view that Gorbachev's renewal of cadres was either intended to promote committed reformers, or was effective in doing so. As long as he remained committed to achieving change through the agency of the Communist Party he was bound to retain senior officials who were representative of its broader views, and he would be hampered in introducing reforms by the resistance of conservative forces that were spread throughout the system. It should be noted, however, that the inbuilt conservatism of the Communist Party may have been at odds with broader social developments. Indeed for some writers, the whole movement for reform and the eventual collapse of the system can be explained in terms of developments in at least some layers of society which had already outstripped the possibilities offered by communism. Historian Catherine Merridale has argued that 'the increasing complexity of society had created new constituencies and demands, and the social pressures generated under Brezhnev would probably have found an outlet of some kind sooner or later'. Highly educated and literate citizens were both more likely to be dissatisfied with the existing regime, and were necessary for reform to work [61: 20]. Sociologist David Lane develops this analysis further. Over time, the process of modernisation induced a number of changes in the Soviet social structure. Among them was the growth of a layer of well-educated and skilled workers, who found that in the conditions of communism, there was an insufficient number of jobs where these skills could be employed. At the same time, the 1960s, 1970s and 1980s witnessed a remarkable growth in the numbers of professionals (engineers, doctors, vets, lawyers, teachers and other service personnel). Members of this social group were denied the relatively higher earnings of their equivalents in the West, and were also more disturbed by the absence of political rights and freedom of speech. Even unskilled manual workers, the traditional base of support for the regime, had expectations of rising living standards which would be hard to satisfy without renewed economic growth. But it was above all the professionals who formed the social basis for reform and who had most to gain from radical change [66]. Many members of this group remained outside or on the fringes of the structures of power, and some even turned to the dissident movement. It seems impossible that their presence could not be felt within the formal structures, and Lane points out that the educational and occupational profile of the members of the Communist Party, the Supreme Soviet, and the Congress of People's Deputies also shifted dramatically in the last 30 years of the Soviet Union [66: 107–8]. Even within the official power structures, and especially in some of the regions away from Moscow, a rising political elite shared many of these values and represented a totally different political outlook from the Old Guard [41: 55–8].

If this analysis is correct, then the picture of an unremittingly conservative and anti-reform Communist Party needs to be severely qualified. There was at least tension between the political and material advantages available through loyalty to the old ways and the potential gains available under a free market and democracy. At any rate Gorbachev was either unable or unwilling initially to mobilise this group in support of his reform programme, but the fact that it existed helps explain the later momentum achieved under *glasnost* and is an important consideration in assessing the balance between liberals and conservatives which will be addressed in Chapter 11.

8 Economic Reforms

The state of the economy dominated Gorbachev's early reform programme. Before 1985, there appeared to be no threat to the system of one-party rule which had served the leadership well since Lenin's time, there was no reason to suppose that national relations were anything but harmonious, and the Soviet Union even appeared to be living in a stable international environment in spite of the 1979 invasion of Afghanistan and the more aggressive attitude of Ronald Reagan's administration in the USA. But as shown in Chapter 3, the economy was giving increasing cause for concern. It was only after the failure of his early attempts to revive the economy that Gorbachev understood the links between economic performance and deeper social and political factors, leading him to consider more radical changes which, to his dismay, not only upset irretrievably the apparent stability he had inherited, but also precipitated a far more rapid downward spiral in the economy.

Although major concerns about the performance of the economy had been raised in the 'Novosibirsk Report', prepared by the leading economic sociologist Tatiana Zaslavskaia, in 1983, it seems that by and large the Soviet leadership were still unaware of the depths of the country's economic problems, and were optimistic about its future [71: *13*]. As late as 1988, Gorbachev's chief economic adviser Abel Agenbegyan agreed with official forecasts of recovery to an annual growth rate of 4–5 per cent by 2000, and confidently predicted that the Soviet Union would overtake the USA in terms of productivity, efficiency and quality by the time of the centenary of the Russian Revolution [68: *2–6, 40*]. This process of acceleration (*uskorenie*) was to be achieved by a series of piecemeal reforms and shifts in priority, for example, increasing levels of investment, which could be undertaken within the confines of the existing system.

Table 8.1 Competing estimates of Soviet national income economic growth, 1928–87 (percentage change per year)

	Official Soviet figures	CIA estimates	Soviet economist G.I. Khanin
1928–40	13.9	6.1	3.2
1940–50	4.8	2.0	1.6
1950–60	10.2	5.2	7.2
1960–65	6.5	4.8	4.4
1965–70	7.7	4.9	4.1
1970–75	5.7	3.0	3.2
1975–80	4.2	1.9	1.0
1980–85	3.5	1.8	0.6
1985–87	3.0	2.7	2.0

Source: [24: *146*].

But official Soviet statistics on the overall state of the economy indicated a sufficient slowdown in the pattern of economic growth, and other estimates suggest that these statistics themselves may have masked the real difficulties faced in the economy (see Table 8.1). Like Khrushchev in an earlier era, Gorbachev recognised the need to shift from 'extensive' to 'intensive' economic growth, and looked to science and technology for the solution [44: *107*]. However, as early as 1986, Gorbachev went further than his predecessor in calling for structural change based not just on the decentralisation of decision-making, but also on the use of market indicators as a measure of performance, and a more responsive price system. These principles were embodied in the 12th Five-Year Plan for 1986–90, introduced at the 27th Congress of the CPSU in February 1986. The Plan optimistically set targets for overall output, productivity and investment, as well as individual targets for key products such as oil, coal and grain substantially higher than the targets for the previous Plan of 1981–85, inspite of the fact that few of these targets had been achieved [22: *183–5*]. To some extent there was sound economic thinking behind the increased priority accorded to updating machinery as a way of improving productivity, but the slowness of the Soviet system to absorb new technology and the unrealistic levels of investment required meant that any benefits of this approach would take several years to materialise, if they were to do so at all [11: *441*].

Short-term improvements in productivity would, then, only be achieved by exhortations, cutting out inefficiency, mismanagement and corruption, and getting workers to work more effectively – the sort of campaign which had been a regular, and failed, feature of attempts at economic reform from Stalin's time onwards. In one area, Gorbachev, urged on by Ligachev, did take concrete steps to eliminate a specific obstacle to higher productivity – alcoholism. Not only did drunkenness at work, and absences resulting from it, make workers less efficient, there were direct costs to the economy associated with high levels of industrial accidents and the pressures placed on the health service. The anti-alcohol campaign introduced in May 1985 saw drastic cuts in the legal production of vodka and wine, the destruction of vineyards and distilleries, a trebling of prices, restrictions on the hours at which alcohol could be sold, a disciplinary crackdown on drunkenness at work and the raising of the legal drinking age to 21. The result was an overall drop in the consumption of alcohol by about a quarter, with some real health benefits and savings [22: *180*]. But there were also drastic negative consequences for the economy. Tax revenues fell leaving an overall shortfall of about 3.5 per cent of the state budget; the substantial reduction of retail sales contributed to inflationary pressures; and finally, much of the shortfall in alcohol production was made up by illegal moon-shining or *samogon*, leading to the growth of a black market which was not subject to state regulation or taxation, placed new burdens on the police, and laid the basis for the emergence of organised crime, as had happened in the USA under prohibition in the 1920s. Whatever the spiritual justification of the campaign, overall its effects on the economy were destabilising [69: *76*].

Like the anti-alcohol campaign, other measures introduced in 1985–86 were not untypical of Soviet attempts at reform, and while they were pursued more vigorously than before, they eventually foundered on the bureaucratic system which was entrusted with implementing them. Commissions were established to grade the quality of finished products with results that were included in the assessment of production figures, but after a while the traditional emphasis on quantity rather than quality prevailed. The creation of 'superministries' to better co-ordinate the activities of particular sectors of the economy ought to have produced some benefits by eliminating wasteful rivalry and lack of communication between smaller ministries, but it failed to introduce any decentralisation in place of the hierarchical direction of economic activity. Gorbachev's attacks against complacency and corruption may have caused some discomfort amongst senior officials, but again such comments were not previously unheard of, and overall there was little to suggest that anything more than tinkering with the system to improve efficiency was being contemplated [22: *189*].

Despite some encouraging signs in 1986, it soon became clear that these adjustments fell far short of what was needed to meet the ambitious plans for economic growth. As a result of the relative openness he had already encouraged, Gorbachev was learning that even the limited measures he had introduced were failing to make any impact as a result of obstruction by officials at the local level. A more radical approach was prompted by figures which indicated that in the first months of 1987 industrial output was failing to increase significantly, and might actually be falling in key sectors. The frustration of the early reform attempts showed that the maintenance of a hierarchical system of economic planning and direction meant that any reforms would run up against the resistance of the bureaucracy which Gorbachev had no choice but to rely on for carrying them out; individuals and organisations concerned were bound to be conservative by nature, and viewed even limited reform as a threat to their own privileges and security. As a result the emphasis in 1987–89 was on decentralising decision-making and responsibility to lower levels, without abandoning central planning altogether or allowing the introduction of market forces to any significant degree. Most notably, while some prices were modified to fall more in line with production costs, the principle of state control of prices was not abandoned.

The key pieces of legislation in this period were decrees allowing the establishment of joint ventures in January 1987, the Law on the State Enterprise of June the same year, and the Law on Cooperatives of May 1988. Joint ventures allowed foreign ownership up to 49 per cent of companies operating in the USSR and were, in part, an attempt to attract foreign investment and make up for the shortfall in foreign currency earnings which were needed to import new machinery and foodstuffs, as well as gradually exposing sections of the economy to western know-how. But the very fact that these ventures were supposed to operate outside of the system of central planning meant that they were starved of materials allocated by the central agencies, while theoretical exemptions from normal regulation (for instance, exemption from import duties on materials) were frequently not observed by officials. All the same, by the end of 1990, there were 2905 joint ventures registered in the Soviet Union, but they were mostly very small and made little impact on the overall economy.

The Law on the State Enterprise had more far-reaching implications. It allowed enterprises more control over their own finances and the ability to dispose off a portion of any revenues generated, some leeway in decision-making over what and how much was produced and the ability to conclude independently contracts and other arrangements with each other, with cooperatives, with the state and with the smaller individual entrepreneurs regarding trade, provision of materials and research and development. Enterprises were not, however, freed altogether from central planning and were still subject to the authority of branch ministries, which also retained the right to allocate the bulk of machinery and raw materials. Real autonomy for enterprises therefore rested very much on the attitude of the planners and ministries, and the tight annual plan targets produced by *Gosplan* for 1988 only served to strengthen the natural inclination of the ministries to keep hold of the maximum directive powers that were permissible.

Arguably the most innovative and most successful of Gorbachev's economic reforms was the establishment of cooperatives. By allowing groups of people on their own initiative to form enterprises which, while still subject to regulation by the state, effectively operated outside of the centrally planned economy, the reform enabled the emergence of a sector of the economy which could operate according to market forces, was allowed to dispose off its own profits and provided real incentives for both managers and employees to raise productivity. Even if the sector remained relatively small, it could perhaps provide a model for future developments in the economy more generally, and provided an area in which entrepreneurially minded citizens could develop business skills and acumen. As long as the central authorities kept control of the allocation of materials, the cooperative movement was inevitably confined primarily to the service sector. High street businesses such as cafes and hairdressers formed the first cooperatives, followed by small-scale building and transport firms, eventually spreading into an independent banking, market research and information provision sector. Many of the entrepreneurs who first cut their teeth in the cooperatives later went on to play an important role in the post-Soviet economy and government. By 1991, 245,356 cooperatives employed over six million people, and were held to be far more efficient than state enterprises, to the extent that the state frequently contracted out work in construction, for instance, to independent cooperatives.

The movement was however, not without its problems. Their high visibility and profitability made them obvious targets for both legal and illegal harassment and extortion by local authorities and, ultimately, for racketeering and demands for protection money from criminal gangs. The chaotic currency and pricing system created distortions which in turn made it difficult for cooperatives to expand or make long-term plans with any degree of certainty. Under these circumstances it was only natural for successful entrepreneurs involved in cooperatives to increase their wealth in the short-term rather than investing to expand or improve. The existence of this semi-liberalised sector alongside the planned economy also led to abuses: it became common for state enterprises to use 'attached cooperatives' to sell their products at uncontrolled prices, with relatives or close allies of the enterprise manager running the cooperative and ensuring that the manager took a share of the profits. Without further decentralisation of the economy, it was impossible for the model to extend significantly out of services and into production. In any case, even under the most favourable of circumstances, it was unlikely that such a model could be applied to large-scale industry in any recognisable form [22: *194–209*].

Looked at in isolation, there was a great deal to be said for each of these reforms, and there is a case to be made that had they been allowed to develop in more favourable political circumstances they might have led to a more radically altered and more efficient economic system eventually. The Soviet economist Abel Agenbegyan explicitly argued that the process of reform which was now known as *perestroika* (restructuring) was a gradual but accelerating process which would take time to come to fruition: 'We believe in *perestroika* and are optimistic. And although it is proceeding slowly, with difficulty, and many mistakes have already been made along the way, with more probably yet to come; nonetheless, as Gorbachev has said, there is nowhere for us to retreat. We must move forward, increasing speed as we go' [68: *44*]. But there were clear problems with such a gradual approach, which attempted to introduce new elements into an environment dominated by old systems and attitudes. Economic reform in 1987–89 foundered on four major obstacles: first, existing institutions at both the local and central levels continued to be dominated by personnel who were either apathetic or actively hostile to reform, and could use their positions to hinder it; second, the maintenance of the key elements of central planning, and in particular the frequently arbitrary system whereby most prices were determined directly by the planning agencies, restricted the opportunities for development of independent or decentralised enterprises; third, the reforms were introduced as piecemeal reactions to particular problems or as individual brainchilds conceived and implemented in isolation from each other – at this stage there was no central long-term vision of reform of any coherence; and fourth, the reforms were introduced at a time when the international environment was generally unfavourable to the performance of the Soviet economy and created specific obstacles to economic growth and successful reform.

This last point deserves some attention, as it gives rise to a line of argument that external factors which were entirely beyond Gorbachev's control were ultimately responsible for economic failure. The Soviet invasion of Afghanistan in 1979 not only proved to be more protracted and costly than had been anticipated, but provoked an unexpected reaction in the form of trading sanctions from the West. Gorbachev also inherited from his predecessors a commitment to match US President Ronald Reagan's Strategic Defence Initiative (SDI) by investing heavily in a comparable programme, a drain on the country's resources which Gorbachev, initially at least, was not inclined to abandon [11: *441*]. A world slump in oil prices dealt a severe blow to the USSR's foreign currency earnings (some 24 billion dollars over five years), while finally, instability and eventually the collapse of communist regimes in Eastern Europe deprived the Soviet Union of previously guaranteed trading partners.

While some of these losses, like the loss of state revenue arising from the anti-alcohol campaign, were the unintended but direct consequences of Soviet policies, others clearly were not, and it has certainly been argued that Gorbachev experienced considerable bad luck in these and other areas just when his reform programme was getting under way [74: *376–7*]. The cumulative financial cost of these factors was not insignificant, and it was partly in response that Gorbachev sought to improve relations with the West (see Chapter 15). In the short term, perhaps the most serious consequence of the US-led embargo was that it denied the Soviet Union access to new technological developments in which Gorbachev had placed so much hope in his early reform efforts [73: 56].

By 1989, it was clear that far from improving, the Soviet economy was slowing to a virtual halt. Most seriously of all, in late 1988 rationing and shortages of basic consumer goods were becoming a common occurrence, bringing with it the very real risk of popular discontent and unrest. Advocates of a more radical reform involving wholesale moves towards market principles now became more vocal. The possibility of market reform had been openly discussed in the Soviet press since 1987. In July 1989 a State Commission on Economic Reform headed by Leonid Abalkin was set up to consider alternative reform strategies. Its staff included a number of economists who later became known as supporters of radical market reform, including Abel Aganbegyan, Stanislav Shatalin, Grigorii Yavlinskii and Evgenii Yasin, and the Commission operated in complete independence of the powerful but conservative state planning agency *Gosplan*. The strategy recommended by the Commission called for a gradual move to a mixed economy which relied heavily on market forces while retaining elements of socialist control. Characteristically, Gorbachev vacillated over its implementation. The Prime Minister Nikolai Ryzhkov, although initially supportive of Abalkin, announced a two-year delay in starting reform in December 1989. Shortly afterwards, with Gorbachev's encouragement, a more radical and rapid reform plan was drawn up, only to be rejected because it included forecasts of short-term falls in real income and rises in unemployment, similar to those being experienced under Poland's shock therapy programme at the same time. In May 1990, Ryzhkov announced a revised plan whereby prices would be raised in order to reduce inflationary pressures but not liberalised. In October, Shatalin published his '500 Days Programme' under which privatisation and the removal of price controls would be achieved rapidly, with the main elements of the reform to be completed by February 1992. The plan was accepted by the parliament of the Russian Federation, now under Yeltsin's leadership, but rejected by the government of the USSR, which opted instead for a considerably watered down version.

The result was chaos. The federal USSR and its constituent republics, most importantly, the Russian Federation, were now pursuing incompatible economic programmes. Much of the 'war of laws' between the Soviet and Russian governments revolved around the issue of which controlled the land and other assets located on Russian territory. The Soviet government did introduce some price liberalisation in January 1991, but in a half-hearted manner which was anyway thwarted by non-cooperation and profiteering at the local level. Public finances were by now entirely out of control and the soaring budget deficit fuelled inflation and eroded the value of savings. The economy was in free-fall: on the most reliable estimates, Soviet output fell by nearly a fifth over the two years 1990–91 [22: *236–7*]. Shortages of meat and dairy products became endemic, queuing for basic foodstuffs became an everyday feature of Soviet life and rationing proved ineffective when even goods to which the ration-card holders were entitled were not available. The black market, in both currency trading and the provision of goods, flourished, but was not sufficient to hold off the real fall in living standards experienced by Soviet citizens.

It is impossible to judge whether either gradual or wholesale market reform could have saved the Soviet economy from collapse, since neither strategy was consistently applied at any time. The ultimately successful transition in countries like Poland and Czechoslovakia provides few clues, as it was achieved together with the dismantling of the communist system and involved short-term costs that may have been unacceptable in the circumstances faced by Gorbachev. The example of China is frequently held up to show how a communist regime could successfully adapt to the market. However, the Chinese reform programme involved a level of control, both by the state over the population, and by the leadership over the state, which had long ceased to be available to Gorbachev. His dilemma was that even moderate reform faced obstruction at all levels from *Gosplan* and the ministries down to individual enterprise managers, who saw their privileges and long-established certainties under threat. On the other hand, the prospect of rapidly rising prices and unemployment engendered risks of popular unrest similar to those witnessed in Poland in 1980, risks the regime was not prepared to accept. Finally, however much market reforms might be dressed up in socialist terminology, the adoption of capitalist relations in any form was so much at odds with the fundamental principles of communism that it threatened to undermine altogether the legitimacy of the system and may have been personally unacceptable to Gorbachev himself (see Chapter 6).

To many commentators, economic difficulties both lay at the root of Gorbachev's reform programme and were his eventual undoing. As Ronald Suny puts it: 'Gorbachev's success or failure depended from the beginning on the ability of his administration to get the stagnant Soviet economy moving again' [12: *453*]. The consideration underpinning such a view is that, since the abandonment of repression as the main means of social control in the 1950s, a form of social contract had resulted in passive acceptance of the political monopoly of the CPSU and the absence of political freedoms and rights in exchange for improving standards of living and a high level of provision of public services like education and healthcare. Economic slowdown in the early 1980s threatened to make it impossible for the state to uphold its part of the bargain, and therefore some sort of reform was needed. Once bureaucratic resistance and corruption were identified as major obstacles to improvements in economic performance, Gorbachev was forced to adopt *glasnost* and mobilise popular criticism in the name of reform. This only made him more vulnerable to the pressures from below once the deterioration of the economy started to accelerate, and the loss of economic security spelt his doom. Economic collapse both destroyed popular legitimacy (such as it was) and alienated the traditional *nomenklatura* bastions of the regime, leaving Gorbachev and the whole communist system prey to either reaction, exemplified by the August 1991 coup, or the anti-communist opposition led by Yeltsin.

However, the economist Philip Hanson insists that the collapse of communism was essentially a political phenomenon. Indeed, far from being the cause of political disequilibrium, the economy was actually the victim of politics. In addition to the contradictory political pressures on the reform process already noted, Hanson highlights in particular the tensions between the USSR and the republics which led to incompatible policies being simultaneously pursued and ultimately to a 'systemic vacuum' [22: *227–36, 253–4*]. Ellman and Kontorovich, in a study based on interviews with leading participants in the reform process, concur, adding a number of other political factors which undermined both the economy and the Soviet system: 'the USSR was killed, against the wishes of its ruler, by politics, not economics' [71: *26*]. Mark Harrison adopts a more long-term perspective: the growing complexity of Soviet society made it increasingly difficult for the state to monitor the society and to operate the system of punishments and rewards on which the centrally planned economy depended. Thus the political and economic chaos of the Gorbachev era represented only an acceleration of a process which was embedded in the system and had been going on for a long time [72]. This suggests one way of directly linking political and economic decline, a link which most non-economists tend to take for granted. But from the ancient to the modern world, there are plenty of examples of regimes surviving economic decline or sharp downturns, which reinforces the arguments of Hanson and Ellman and Kontorovich that, while economics and politics were closely intertwined, the economy on its own cannot explain the Soviet collapse.

9 Structural and Constitutional Reform

The preceding two chapters, on personnel changes and the economy, have already made abundantly clear one of the central dilemmas facing Mikhail Gorbachev: once he had decided to embark on a course of reform, he had to rely for its implementation on the institutions which he had inherited and to which he owed his own position – the CPSU and the government, ministries, planning agencies and Soviets of the state. The fact that senior members of both were one and the same people seemed to preclude the possibility of playing off one against the other. While it was possible to take some steps to alter their character through the personnel changes outlined in Chapter 7, the vastness of these organisations and their conservatism made it unlikely that these bodies could ever be won over to give whole-hearted support to the reform programme. Ultimately, as his programme gathered momentum, Gorbachev sought to bypass them by appealing directly to public pressure through the processes of *glasnost* and *demokratizatsiia* (openness and democratisation). Before moving onto these themes in the next chapter, it is worth considering steps to reform the existing institutions, and whether Gorbachev had any real alternatives on offer.

Early approaches to institutional reform can be summarised as consisting of three general tasks: first, the separation and clear definition of the functions of the CPSU on the one hand, and the governmental apparatus on the other; second, streamlining and improving the efficiency of both sets of institutions; and third, eliminating corruption, graft and nepotism. A fourth task which had historically been addressed by the communist leadership was the settlement of questions of regional administration and centre–local relations. Under Gorbachev, this challenge came down mostly to the question of the status of the federal relations between the USSR and its 15 constituent republics.

Disentangling the Party from the State was no easy task. Through a set of unwritten but widely recognised rules, the bonds between the two were linked in the system of appointments from the very top-down: certain ministerial portfolios and the leadership of agencies such as the KGB more or less guaranteed membership of the CPSU's supreme body, the Politburo. In the highest legislative body, the Supreme Soviet, according to one study, 39 per cent of deputies 'elected' in 1984 were *ex officio* appointments based on their position in the Party and State hierarchy [44: 35]. To all appearances, it was the Party which controlled appointments and was therefore the real power behind the State, although in reality the system was so intermeshed that it was possible to rise through the state bureaucracy and obtain promotion in the Party as a result, or vice-versa. From one perspective, this was not really a problem. In Western democracies, it is common for responsible appointments from ministerial level downwards to be allocated to the senior members of the party or coalition that has achieved electoral success. True, they are usually backed up by an independent civil service which can smooth the transition from one government to another, but such considerations were of little relevance to a one-Party state. Indeed, the problem was rather that where the personnel were not identical, there might be two or more bodies dealing with the same matter, duplicating functions or sending out contradictory instructions.

In fact, at the 19th Conference of the CPSU in June–July 1988, Gorbachev put forward the idea of combining the posts of First Secretary of the Party in each region and district with that of Chairman of the Soviet of People's Deputies of the same territory – although this would have meant little more than acknowledging what already existed in practice [13: 465]. In October of the same year, he gained the title of President of the USSR in conjunction with his job of leader of the Party. Thus Gorbachev's concern was not so much over the division of personnel between the authoritative bodies of the Party and State, as with the task, as laid out by the 19th Party Conference, 'to delimit the functions of the party and the state' [59: 47]. This was to be achieved by strengthening the

Soviets financially, allowing deputies greater independence and security (being elected for five years rather than the existing two and a half years) and restricting the ability of the CPSU to control and discipline delegates [44: *36*]. The reorganised policy sections of the Central Committee of the CPSU would deal only with 'the most important questions' without 'interfering in detail with the practical work of the state's organs'. Analogous reforms were to be introduced at the regional and Republican levels [59: *47–8*].

These measures towards separation were accompanied by a reduction in the number of CC departments with responsibility for particular areas of policy, from 20 to 9, and the creation of 6 new commissions. Only two of the sections with direct responsibility for economic management, those for 'Economic and Social Issues' and 'Agriculture' were retained. Gorbachev aimed to reduce bureaucracy and malco-ordination at the top level by cutting the number of officials employed in the CC apparatus from nearly 2000 to closer to 1000 [60: *120*]. The streamlining of the State apparatus was already in progress by this stage. As early as November 1985 five ministries and a committee were merged into a single body responsible for overseeing agricultural production – the *Gosagroprom*. The creation of 'superministries' to co-ordinate efforts at economic reform has been mentioned in the preceding chapter.

Relatively little attention has been paid to these structural changes – understandably so, since any effect they were expected to produce were soon overwhelmed by the far more fundamental changes accompanying *demokratizatsiia*. It should be noted, however, that lack of clarity in the first place over the structure of power may have contributed to the chaos that followed *demokratizatsiia*. The changes to party statutes adopted in September 1988 were vague and elusive on the exact structure [59: *48*], while constitutional amendments aimed at separating the party from the state failed to clarify the equally important but different separation of powers between the legislative and executive branches of government [56: *112*]. The reorganisation and division of powers between the Party and State apparatuses ought to have clarified which set of institutions were to provide the real motor for the reform programme, but on this question political scientists and historians are divided. Writing at the time, Archie Brown claimed that the reduction in number of CC departments 'represented a considerable strengthening of Gorbachev's personal position' by allowing him greater scope to supervise the work of the departments and to reinforce the commitment to *perestroika* through personnel changes [60: *120*]. But Stephen White concludes that the institutional reforms represented 'more generally a shift of executive authority from party to state institutions' [44: *34–5*]. Martin McCauley goes further, citing Nikolai Ryzhkov in support of the view that, inspite of Gorbachev's intentions, the power of the Party suffered a rapid decline after 1988, and with it Gorbachev's personal authority, leaving him to fall back on his position as head of state [56: *112*]. Robert Service contends that this shift was not accidental or unforeseen, but the result of a deliberate move by Gorbachev at the time of the June 1988 Party conference: 'The party was being dropped as the vanguard of *perestroika*' [11: *462*]. For Dmitri Volkogonov, on the other hand, Gorbachev sought to promote his reform programme through strengthening his control of the CPSU and defending its constitutional role [13: *465–6*].

Like most of Gorbachev's reforms, the restructuring of authority was implemented in an *ad hoc* and unco-ordinated manner. While the streamlining of the apparatus may have eliminated some waste and simplified the decision-making process, it simultaneously introduced new contradictions and tensions. The creation of a new body, the Congress of People's Deputies, introduced another element into the system which opened the door to more confusion and competition for authority.

The lack of agreement over how Gorbachev sought to utilise existing institutions reflects both the uncertainty of his own course and the ineffectiveness of such institutional measures. Whatever steps he tried to take, Gorbachev was confronted with a vast bureaucratic apparatus whose cooperation had to be secured, by one means or another, if his reform programme was to be effective at all. While it was always possible to promote reformers into leading positions this in itself would not remove the obstacles thrown up at all levels by conservative, privileged and frequently corrupt officials. The more salacious details of corruption and privilege are a favourite topic of journalistic accounts of the period [45: *180–94*]. Corruption, as we have seen (Chapter 5) was a major target of Yuri Andropov's rule, and as a result Gorbachev inherited a more favourable situation than might have been. Gorbachev used personnel changes to root out some of the remaining worst offenders – Dinmukhamed Kunaev,

Geidar Aliyev and Vladimir Shcherbitsky most prominent among them – and in the most public sign of a clampdown on corruption, in December 1988 Brezhnev's son-in-law Yuri Churbanov, a former deputy chief of the Ministry of the Interior, was sentenced to 12 years imprisonment for graft.

But while such demonstrative measures might have been effective in eliminating the most serious cases of overt corruption, they had little impact on those members of the bureaucracy who, whether staying within the bounds of legality or not, perceived their interests as being so caught up in the preservation of the existing system that they had every incentive to obstruct reform. At the same time, the decline in central control over the regions and a loosening of economic regulation contributed to an atmosphere where corruption might be able to flourish unchecked [11: *466*].

Moves against corrupt party and state officials, while generally popular among the population at large, carried with them their own dangers. Corrupt individuals did not operate in isolation. In the regions they had, over a number of years, built-up loyal followings, often compared to Mafiosi, who could benefit from a share of the privileges of power, and could cause problems for the central authorities even when their patrons had been removed. The difficulty was exacerbated in the non-Russian republics, where long-serving leaders had promoted national and even clan identities in order to buttress their positions. Any move against them could therefore be portrayed as an assault on national rights. Having removed Dinmukhamed Kunayev as First Secretary of the Communist Party of Kazakhstan in December 1986, Gorbachev aggravated the situation by appointing as his successor an ethnic Russian, Gennadii Kolbin. In response a number of Kazakhs rioted for several days in the capital Almaty, leading to the death of up to 250 protestors and members of the security forces. The protests may well have been co-ordinated by supporters of Kunaev, but they also reflected the inherent explosiveness of the national question [82: *552*]. The potential for strife in the republics was exacerbated by the erosion of central authority which accompanied Gorbachev's political reforms [12: *457*].

The Kazakh riots may have opened Gorbachev's eyes for the first time to the importance of the national question in the Soviet Union, although conflicts between Russians and Yakuts in Yakutia in June 1986 had already shaken the complacency and confidence of the Soviet leadership over national relations. That Gorbachev shared this complacency was apparent from comments he made shortly after assuming the post of General Secretary, when he declared that Soviet socialism had definitively resolved the question of nationality and that the population of the Soviet Union was 'a single family – the Soviet people'. Once the realisation had dawned that a combination of political and economic decentralisation together with *glasnost* led to the emergence of the republics as key bases of power and encouraged the articulation of a range of national demands, reform of the federal structure of the USSR became the key constitutional project of the final years of Gorbachev's rule. His initial approach, lasting through to 1989, was to call for the development of economic ties between the republics, fostering local languages and cultures, while in other ways the national question would be satisfied by the broader evolution of democracy and economic reform. The only significant constitutional change in this time was the creation in 1988 of a Council of the Federation attached to the Supreme Soviet of the USSR. It had little more than consultative powers, however [56: *166*], and proved ineffective at assuaging the centrifugal forces which were already threatening to tear the Federation apart.

The importance of the national question was recognised by a decision to convene a special meeting of the CC on the matter, but the fact that it was postponed no fewer than four times indicates both the complexity of the question and the indecisiveness of the leadership in choosing which line to pursue [79: *367*]. By the time the CC plenum did meet, in September 1989, events had spiralled out of control to the extent that its decisions made little real impact [44: *176*]. The eruption of national movements and the willingness of republican leaders to exploit them had far outstripped the ability of constitutional tinkering to contain them, as discussed in Chapter 12. Seeking a more radical solution, Gorbachev published a draft of a new Union Treaty in November 1990, organised a partially successful referendum on the future of the Union in March 1991 and was engaged in work on a revised version of the Treaty at the time of the attempted coup of August 1991. The purpose of the Union Treaty would have been to put the relationship between the republics and the centre on a new footing, that was more favourable to the republics than the old constitution. But as the republics had already acquired considerable powers in the years 1989–91, and with some of them threatening to break away regardless, Gorbachev had little with which to bargain except economic favours, which could hardly be delivered at that time of economic collapse. All the same Gorbachev had displayed admirable skill in getting the plan past conservative opponents in the USSR. Buoyed by the referendum result and the engagement of the leaders of most of the republics, he may have had good reason for optimism concerning keeping at least a reduced Soviet Union together, before events overtook the process [34: *152*].

Nevertheless, Gorbachev's failure to control the republics, and the willingness of his chief rival, Yeltsin, to exploit national divisions (see Chapter 16) were major factors not only in the break up of the USSR but in discrediting and rendering the whole system of communism unmanageable. The explosion of national unrest from 1988 onwards was largely unpredicted and unexpected. This fact has not prevented subsequent criticism of Gorbachev for complacency and casualness in this area [11: *455–6*]. A more far-sighted leader might not only have recognised the need to keep the republics on his side, but might even have seen the possibility of harnessing the more progressive intellectual and political forces in the republics as important allies in the reform process against the more conservative tendencies in the central party and state apparatus. Some recognition of these possibilities can be seen in the early efforts to introduce market-style reforms earlier than elsewhere in the Baltic republics, where resistance might be expected to be less wholehearted [70: *168–9*]. But in doing so Gorbachev only succeeded in giving encouragement to radicals who were later to spearhead the Popular Front movements in the region. The dilemma for Gorbachev was that, unlike Yeltsin, he was deeply committed to preserving the integrity of the USSR and this hampered his ability to exploit possible divisions within the federation. Concession soon turned to repression in the Baltic republics as a result, contributing in no small way to the eventual demise of the Federation. Finally, Gorbachev can be criticised for being too slow to recognise that the independence of the Baltic states was perhaps inevitable in any case, and for failing to take adequate steps to pursue an alternative option of preserving the Union of the remaining 12 republics.

There exists a broad consensus that, while mistakes were made and individual reforms were ill-thought out, thorough reform of the bureaucracy without the more radical measures involved in *demokratizatsiia* was, in practice, a futile exercise. What can be called into question is the wisdom of embarking on political and economic reform simultaneously [34: *159*]. The Chinese example suggests that successful economic reform could be achieved within the framework of communism so long as a tight grip was kept on the Party and there was a readiness to implement repression ruthlessly. But could Gorbachev have followed the Chinese path? Arguably it was too late to go for the sort of piecemeal gradual reform which allowed the Chinese communists to retain control, and in the Soviet case it was the obstructiveness of the ruling party which necessitated some sort of political shake-up in tandem with economic reform. However, it is worth noting that, although he was forced to make compromises and bow to conservatism at a number of key junctures, most of the time Gorbachev was remarkably successful in getting innovative and uncomfortable measures accepted by the CC of the CPSU and other bodies. It is conceivable that with a bit more patience, and without the economy on the verge of collapse, reform of and through the party–state apparatus might have succeeded over time. As it was, Gorbachev chose, in effect, to partially abandon this path by moving outside the established institutions.

10 *Glasnost* and Democratisation

On 26 April 1986, the core of a reactor at a nuclear power station in the Ukrainian town of Chernobyl overheated, setting off the worst nuclear accident in history to date. Radioactive fallout spread far enough to be detected in Scandinavia and Poland. As a result, the news that a major nuclear incident had occurred somewhere in the Soviet Union was known to the rest of the world before it reached the Soviet population. When, three days later, the Soviet authorities finally released some information to foreign embassies and news agencies, and eventually to their own people, they suggested that the incident was minor and had been effectively contained [13: *479*]. A year later, in May 1987, an eccentric young German, Mathias Rust, flew his light plane across Soviet space, evading the radar and defence systems of one of the world's two great superpowers, and landed next to the Kremlin in Moscow's Red Square.

It appears that these two incidents played a major part in triggering Gorbachev's policy of *glasnost*, or openness. According to Robert Service, '... the Chernobyl nuclear explosion undoubtedly had a deep impact on [Gorbachev]' [11: *446*]. Martin McCauley makes the link even more explicit: 'Glasnost became essential after the poor handling of the Chernobyl nuclear disaster ... The reaction of the public demonstrated that the official media enjoyed little credibility' [56: *64*]. Volkogonov interprets the impact of the disaster less in terms of popular reaction and more in terms of the international impression Gorbachev was already trying to make: 'It seems that it was not long after the explosion at Chernobyl that Gorbachev came to understand the power of world opinion' [13: *480*]. But it does not seem altogether sufficient to view *glasnost* simply as an immediate response to these events. Gorbachev had already employed the term in addresses in December 1984 and February 1985, although little notice was taken at the time. We have already seen that by early 1987 it was clear that administrative and exhortational strategies were failing to produce the required impact, and there are signs that frustration over the possibilities for reform had set in even before Chernobyl. The first example of *glasnost* cited by both Stephen White and Ronald Suny was a mild criticism of the Brezhnev era at the 27th CPSU Congress in February 1986 [44: *77*, 12: *452*].

Mike Haynes argues that an equal factor in promoting *glasnost* was the evidence of inertia in the system and the possibility that 'even moderate reform would again be suffocated as it had been in the past' [7: *197*]. Certainly there were more deep-seated reasons for such a policy. But it does seem that the Chernobyl incident, in particular, added immediate impetus to the process. In June 1986 *Glavlit* (the Main Administration for Affairs of Literature and Publishing Houses) and the Union of Writers were instructed to relax rules on censorship, and by the end of the year three newspapers, *Moscow News*, *Ogonek* and *Arguments and Facts*, were expressing relatively radical opinions under the guidance of newly appointed editors. Films, plays and books which were critical or satirical of the Soviet system were released for the first time or were newly composed. In a more public and dramatic gesture, in December 1986 Gorbachev responded to a set of complaints from the dissident physicist Andrei Sakharov by speaking to him personally over the telephone and inviting him to return to Moscow. Sakharov's support for human rights and freedom of speech had made him a thorn in the establishment's side since Khrushchev's time, and since 1980 he had been subject to house arrest in the town of Gorki, from where he continued to bombard the leadership with demands. His case had become an international *cause celebre*, and his release immediately raised Gorbachev's stock in the estimation of politicians and commentators in the West, who now for the first time began to suspect that something truly different was happening in the USSR. Surely Gorbachev would have been aware of the international impact of his gesture [13: *471*]. But when the release of Sakharov is put alongside other measures like the relaxation of censorship, which had been less widely noted, it would seem that it was also intended to have an impact at home. The move was a clear sign of a rapidly changing atmosphere – Gorbachev had published highly critical remarks of Sakharov as recently as February 1986 in the French newspaper *L'Humanité*.

The particular constituency which Gorbachev was initially appealing to was the intelligentsia. Suny views the early examples of *glasnost* as a direct result of the need to find new allies in society, which could be achieved by defining 'a new relationship between the party and the intelligentsia' [12: *454*]. As Gorbachev came around to the realisation that more fundamental reforms would be needed to get the economy going and revitalise Soviet society, it became equally clear at the same time that any such measures would face resistance. To some extent this could be weakened or overcome by the appointment of supporters of reform to senior positions, but the pool from which such individuals like Boris Yeltsin and Alexander Yakovlev could be found for promotion within the Communist system was limited, and in any case the impossibility of using the powers of appointment to change the massive bureaucracy at every level has already been noted. Reform-minded thinkers like the journalist Yegor Yakovlev, sociologist Tatiana Zaslavskaia and the economists Abel Aganbegyan and Oleg Bogomolov had, either out of conscience or as a result of official disapproval, worked on the margins of the system and outside of the *nomenklatura*. They were needed not just to make up the numbers against the pressures of the conservatives, but also because they were the people most capable of coming up with radical and workable solutions to the problems faced by the country, as Zaslavskaia had already done in her 1983 Novosibirsk report on the failings of the command economy [11: *449–50*].

Initially *glasnost* seems to have been aimed at this particular constituency and not at the public at large. A further reason for *glasnost* was that one of the things revealed by Chernobyl was that inadequate information was reaching even the senior leadership in the Politburo. These were limited aims which could be seen as strengthening Gorbachev's own position and ability to act within the existing system, not as a way of dismantling it. It should be noted that at this stage *glasnost* was strictly limited. Censorship was loosened but not abolished, and the Politburo retained the ability to decide what information should be released. Although Sakharov was freed, this was only allowed on condition that he agreed to play no public role in political debate, while other lesser known dissidents remained without freedom. The KGB continued to monitor and harass potential opponents of the regime. And there was no sign yet of any reform of the sham electoral system or any other form of genuine public accountability. 'Openness' is a relative term, and in this case it fell well short of freedom of speech or accountable government.

But there were two problems associated with the introduction of this limited *glasnost*. First, it soon became clear that it was insufficient to achieve any of the aims already discussed. Second, the limited opening up of discussion in the media evoked a reaction in the public at large which might have been anticipated, but apparently was not. The limited nature of reform led many dissidents, led by Sakharov, to remain resolutely opposed to Gorbachev. More broadly the mobilised intelligentsia, rather than offering their direct support to Gorbachev, used the opportunities presented by *glasnost* to address a range of issues according to their own personal agendas. Frustration at the lack of progress led even reforming communists to increasing disillusionment. Yeltsin's dramatic denunciation of Ligachev and criticisms of Gorbachev in front of the CC in October 1987 illustrated this in the starkest terms, removing the most consistent supporter of reform from the highest level of the Party. Although Yeltsin appeared an isolated figure at the time, his subsequent resurgence demonstrated that he was by no means alone in his reservations. While Gorbachev did manage to retain the support of other key allies in the Politburo and at lower levels, it was not sufficient to provide enough backing for a consistent line of reform, as we see in the next chapter. Even where Gorbachev was successful in gaining assent for particular reforms, the failure of his measures to precipitate significant improvements was at least in part blamed on resistance or indifference when it came to implementing them on the ground. Gorbachev's struggle with the conservatives and the need to expose inefficiency, obstruction and corruption at the local level led to an extension of political *glasnost* to the Communist Party. This was most evident at the 19th Party Conference in June–July 1988, which was broadcast on public television. Speakers dwelt on poverty in the countryside, inefficiency in industry, the inadequacy of social services and castigated the leadership, including Gorbachev. Even the recent outcast Boris Yeltsin was eventually allowed to speak, and renewed his assault on the privileges of the Party leadership and the conservatism of older members of the Politburo.

Soviet citizens responded to the new circumstances by increasing magazine subscriptions, queuing to see previously banned films and buying books which were now available for the first time. The encouragement accorded to writers to be more forthcoming in their comments on contemporary issues was seized upon by rock stars and others who had access to wider audiences, especially among the youth. From 1987 onwards, small associations known as *neformaly* or 'informals' began to appear in Moscow and soon spread to other cities. The *neformaly* discussed politics or organised around specific issues, and their total membership numbered over two million by 1990 [11: *475–7*, 7: *198–9*]. This largely unintended mobilisation of popular interest laid the basis for the emergence of larger political, environmental, national and workers' movements described in Part Three. Initially as well as later, these movements were at their strongest in the non-Russian republics. In Russia itself, the consumption of new ideas rarely led to popular activity which might be perceived as presenting any direct threat to the regime or its programme. But the broader reaction to *glasnost* was sufficient to provide it with its own impetus.

The further development of *glasnost* transformed it into the process of *demokratizatsiia* – democratisation. Gorbachev first mooted the idea of secret ballots for multiple candidates during an attack on the stagnation of the CPSU at a Plenum of the Central Committee in January 1987. A limited experiment in multi-candidate elections took place in selected areas for local soviets the following June. But the most significant plan for the extension of democracy on a national scale was announced by Gorbachev at the very end of the 19th Party Conference in June–July 1988. This was the proposal to create a new USSR Congress of People's Deputies, whose members were to be elected partly by public organisations and partly directly by ordinary voters. The Congress would meet once a year, and would itself choose a permanent Supreme Soviet which was to exercise a supervisory role over the government independent of the Party. Some points of the proposal were unclear, including the precise nature of the elections, others were disputed at the conference. But the proposal was passed nonetheless. It took almost a year to clarify procedures, and even then practices varied enormously between localities and organisations. The Communist

Party nominated 100 candidates for the 100 seats that were due to them, as did a number of the other 'social organisations' which were entitled to choose their own deputies. Others, like the trade unions and the Writers' Union, offered more candidates than they were allocated seats, giving their members at least some choice. In the constituencies for popular elections there were also great variations. The Communist Party was the only legal party, and it was clearly expected to control the nominations process. In 384 of the 1500 constituencies, only a single candidate was nominated. Elsewhere, up to 12 candidates contested a single seat.

Even before voting took place, the process of selection of candidates itself proved an eye-opener both to participants and to outside observers. This was, after all, the first time since the 1920s that the Soviet public had any say at all in who would run the country. Even though the Communist Party managed for the most part to keep control of the process, the popular hunger for a freer choice and a deepening of democratisation was clearly evident. Journalist David Remnick witnessed first-hand a nomination meeting at a machine-tool factory in Moscow where, although the officially backed candidate, the factory director, was chosen in the absence of any other proposed candidates, the organisers of the meeting were so taken aback by the vehemence of the opposition and the demands for a more open system that they lost control of the meeting [45: 219]. Similar scenes were reported throughout the country as people displayed their enthusiasm for genuine elections. And the Communist Party establishment did not always get its way. In the choice of candidates for the Russian Academy of Sciences, Andrei Sakharov and others were originally excluded from the approved list, only to be added later in the wake of a concerted campaign by liberals. In spite of rejection by the Communist Party and being denied the means to publicise his candidature, Boris Yeltsin managed to secure nomination as a candidate for the city of Moscow.

The elections themselves, held in March 1989, proved even more of a blow to the establishment. The turnout of 89.8 per cent of electors made this a genuinely representative election wherever a real choice was offered. Voters expressed their disapproval by rejecting high-ranking officials in a number of areas. The Prime Ministers of Latvia and Lithuania and the mayors of Moscow and Kiev were defeated, along with 38 regional party secretaries and the first secretaries of a number of major cities. Yeltsin secured 89.4 per cent of the popular vote in Moscow, while in the second city of Leningrad, the regional first and second Party secretaries, the city Party secretary, the chairman of the regional soviet and the chairman and deputy chairman of the city soviet were all rejected by voters. Other than Yeltsin, Sakharov and other eminent liberal academics and intellectuals, the successful candidates included five religious leaders. Eighty-eight per cent of delegates elected were members of the Communist Party, and the spectacular defeat of important officials needs to be balanced alongside successes for the establishment elsewhere. The whole process had, after all, not been intended as an exercise in a fully free democracy. The result was something of a mix, with Gorbachev able to claim a victory for supporters of his reform programme, but vulnerable to attack at the Congress from independent liberals on the one side and conservative communists on the other.

Whatever their outcome, commentators at the time and later have agreed that the elections were of enormous importance in mobilising the population and providing Soviet citizens with a significant taste of democracy. However, interpretations vary on the three key questions concerning *glasnost* and *demokratizatsiia*: what were Gorbachev's reasons for calling the elections; how democratic were they in reality; and what were the consequences of the exercise? Robert Strayer lists three principal arguments for *glasnost*: the need for more reliable and open information if economic reform was to be successful; the realisation that Soviet society had become increasingly alienated from the Party and the State; and Gorbachev's quest for allies in order to overcome the resistance of the conservative leadership. The development of *glasnost* into *demokratizatsiia* sprung from similar considerations: an attempt to push the Party in the direction of support for more radical reform; and the need to mobilise broader sections of society in order to achieve the successful implementation of those reforms. Strayer adds a further consideration – Gorbachev's belief that he was restoring the particular form of democracy which had been introduced by Lenin and then subverted beyond recognition by Stalin [5: *99, 106*].

Other writers differ as to the emphasis they put on each of these considerations. For White, *glasnost* was primarily about the need to improve information, while *demokratizatsiia* 'was also intended to release the political energies that, for Gorbachev, had been choked off by the bureaucratic centralisation that developed during the Stalin years' [6: *67*]. On this historical note, Service adds that the particular form the Congress of People's Deputies took would have appealed to Gorbachev's rose-tinted view of how mass political gatherings looked in Lenin's time, a perspective which can also help to explain the limited, by Western standards, democratic form the elections took [11: *474*]. Not only was there just one legal Party, a third of delegates were chosen by 'social organisations', and of the others elected by single constituencies many were elected as the only officially approved candidates. The fear of political repression against opponents of the regime had not entirely disappeared either. As late as 7 May 1988, when 100 dissidents formed the organisation 'Democratic Forum' in Moscow in order to contest elections, 5 of its leading members were immediately arrested. The limited nature of the elections was criticised by Russian liberals and Western commentators alike at the time, and even more so later on. In comparison with parliamentary elections in West European democracies, this was certainly a peculiar system. However, Archie Brown, generally the most ardent defender of Gorbachev, points out with some justification that the elections need to be viewed not just in the perspective of centuries of Russian history, but in the specific circumstances of the time: 'It is difficult to see why anyone should have expected Russia to move from extreme authoritarianism and pseudo-elections to fully-fledged democracy and totally free elections in one fell swoop' [54: *181*].

For both McCauley and Service, the aim of both *glasnost* and *demokratizatsiia* was clear: they were intended to mobilise support for reform in the face of the conservative opposition which had hampered earlier efforts, and to secure Gorbachev's own popular approval and authority [56: *263*, 11: *466*]. The consequence implied by this, and here all writers are agreed, was that *demokratizatsiia* undermined irrevocably the authority that had been enjoyed by the CPSU over the past 70 years. There is less of a consensus, however, as to whether this consequence was anticipated and deliberately sought by Gorbachev. Brown's view, shared by a majority, is that this tactic was a 'double-edged sword' – by undermining the CPSU, Gorbachev weakened the one established mechanism at his disposal for the implementation of his policies [54: *190*]. Both McCauley and Suny, on the other hand, emphasise that 'there was no pressure from below' to introduce elections, and the former argues that removing the CPSU as the chief pillar of the political and economic system was a conscious decision of the Gorbachev leadership [56: *263*, 12: *462*]. The reasons why either Gorbachev might deliberately have sought this end, or why it may have happened accidentally, are discussed further in the next chapter, while its consequences become apparent in Part Three.

11 Liberals and Conservatives

Throughout the preceding chapters, the struggle between conservatives and liberals has been a recurring theme: Gorbachev used his powers of appointment to strengthen support for his reforms, while at the same time he felt forced to placate political opponents; efforts to restructure the economy caused frequent conflicts between the two wings; political reform aimed either at creating a constitutional framework for resolving these conflicts, or at providing Gorbachev with the personal authority to operate independently of them; and *glasnost* and *demokratizatsiia* sought to strengthen the hand of the reformers. But until almost the very end, neither side gained a decisive upper hand, and Gorbachev himself, while clearly a reformer, appeared on several occasions to take a conservative stance.

The terms 'liberal' and 'conservative' are commonly employed in the literature to describe opposing tendencies within Soviet society and its predominant political organisation, the CPSU. But a number of cautions need to be recognised in the use of the terms. Both terms denote very broad groups, within which there were substantial variations and disagreements. Liberals were supporters of reform, but were not necessarily liberal in the sense of wholehearted support for free-market economics. Nor were all conservatives diehard Brezhnevites resistant to any kind of change. Both tendencies, in fact, could trace precedents in a tradition of dissent within the Communist movement which argued for pluralism and democracy within a framework of Marxism–Leninism, best represented by the prolific writer Roy Medvedev. In fact there is a strong argument that most communists, possibly including Gorbachev, were centrist in the sense that they sought to preserve socialism but accepted the need for certain changes. Battles between conservatives and liberals were fought over particular reforms, and the composition of both camps and the overall balance of forces between them varied according to the particular reform under discussion. Hence individuals could move towards one camp or the other depending on the issue of the day. The most obvious example is Politburo member Yegor Ligachev, who entered the Politburo as a supporter of reform but finally emerged as the key conservative figure until his removal in 1990. There also existed a strong tradition of obedience within the party towards the General Secretary [12: 252], which on the one hand gave Gorbachev a clear edge in pushing through whichever policies he chose to support, but on the other hand made it too easy for him to vacillate and move in contradictory directions without being pulled up. This factor also makes it difficult to characterise the general membership of the CPSU as either conservative, liberal or even centrist. This is not to say that such people lacked independence of thought. The vigorous debates in the Congress of People's Deputies testify to the strength of opinions, even if Gorbachev usually won the final vote.

Nor does Gorbachev's ability on most occasions to command majority support mean that the views of liberals and conservatives were irrelevant. If nothing else, Gorbachev had to rely on others for providing the details of his reform programme. Economists like Abel Agenbegyan, Stanislav Shatalin, Grigorii Yavlinskii, Evgenii Yasin and Yegor Gaidar and the sociologist Tatiana Zaslavskaia played the key role in developing alternative economic strategies and specific reforms, and became more influential as time went on. Alexander Yakovlev has been described as 'the grandfather of *perestroika* and *glasnost*' and was the key architect of many aspects of reform in the Politburo [56: 55].

It took a long time for such people to be established as the dominant force in the leadership. The first major confrontation between liberals and conservatives in the Politburo resulted in a definite victory for the conservatives. Over the summer of 1987 tensions between Yeltsin and Ligachev had been mounting within the Politburo. Yeltsin was increasingly critical of the slow pace of reform, while for his part Ligachev raised concern over Yeltsin's 'populist' stance and the rate at which he was dismissing personnel in the

Moscow City organisations. In September, Yeltsin wrote privately to Gorbachev asking to be released from his positions in the Moscow Party organisation and the Politburo, and aired his reservations over the pace of reform at the Politburo on 15 October. What sealed Yeltsin's political fate in the short term was his temerity in bringing these disagreements to the attention of the full CC at a plenum on 21 October. Here, he not only condemned Ligachev by name, but implied criticisms of Gorbachev himself. Following Gorbachev's lead, one by one members of the CC rose to condemn Yeltsin, while only a single delegate, Georgy Arbatov, offered a half-hearted defence [13: *503–6*]. Yeltsin was dismissed from his Moscow post on 11 November 1987, and from the Politburo on 18 February 1988. Further denunciations and humiliations followed, and it appeared clear that his career as a real influence in politics was at an end.

Perhaps emboldened by the fall of Yeltsin, Ligachev moved onto the offensive in March 1988. While Gorbachev was away on a diplomatic trip to Yugoslavia, an unknown communist from Leningrad, Nina Andreeva, sent a letter to the conservative newspaper *Sovetskaia Rossiia* which bemoaned the denigration of the memory of Stalin, condemned the moral and political confusion of Soviet youth engendered by *glasnost* and attacked in no uncertain terms 'left-liberal socialists', 'refuseniks', 'neo-liberals', 'neo-Slavophiles', environmentalists and others [58]. Ligachev ensured that the letter was published, and called together a meeting of newspaper editors to impress on them the need to rein in attacks on the Soviet past. The Andreeva letter proved a rallying point for conservative forces, and for a few weeks newspapers printed a number of articles in a similar vein. On this occasion, Gorbachev fought back. On his return to Moscow he convened a Politburo meeting to discuss the affair, and was disturbed to find that not only Ligachev and Gromyko, but his own appointees Viktor Chebrikov and Anatoly Lukianov supported much of Andreeva's sentiments. Yakovlev, Ryzhkov, Shevardnadze and Medvedev attacked them, and Yakovlev was mainly responsible for composing a response which was published in *Pravda* on 5 April. In the wake of this affair, Yakovlev was promoted above Ligachev with responsibility for ideology, and from that point these two became the focal point of the liberal and conservative trends at the highest level.

Ligachev and fellow conservatives suffered a series of further blows in the coming year. In September, Ligachev was moved to responsibility for agriculture, Yakovlev took over from Anatoliy Dobrynin as Secretary of Foreign Affairs, and the surviving grandee of the Brezhnev period, Andrei Gromyko, retired as President of the USSR. A more widespread shake-up of the CC of the CPSU followed the results of the March 1989 elections, with the retirement of 72 full members and 24 candidate members of the CC. Ligachev's influence finally all but disappeared with his defeat in the open election to be Gorbachev's deputy in the Party in June 1990.

Up until 1989, the struggle between conservatives and liberals at the highest level was conducted within the Politburo, and its outcome depended largely on Gorbachev's use of his power of appointment and his readiness to push through particular reforms. A direct result of *demokratizatsiia*, however, was that it gave a public platform to supporters of a variety of views. A much more open test of the strength of the two wings took place, then, once the Congress of People's Deputies met in May 1989. Although factions were not formally recognised and CPSU members dominated the Congress, Yeltsin, Sakharov and other radicals formed an Inter-Regional Group with some 300 members out of 2250 deputies. At the other extreme the group *Soyuz* was formed, whose main concern was to preserve the territorial integrity of the Soviet Union and which eventually numbered some 600 deputies in its ranks. This left a majority in between who were either centrist, or instinctively loyal to the General Secretary regardless of their views of his policies.

To some extent, this enabled Gorbachev to act even more independently of either conservatives or liberals than before. He was not dependent on the votes of either, but by providing both factions with an open platform and representation the liberals, in particular, could not complain with any effectiveness that they were being cut out by undemocratic means. Instead they operated as a kind of official Opposition, able to criticise the government, but unable to change its policies. Through a combination of skilful manoeuvering and his command of an outright majority, Gorbachev never lost control of the Congress [56: *108*]. This effective marginalisation of both liberals and conservatives at the Congress served to undermine the role of the CPSU and enhance Gorbachev's personal power, although his constant exposure to criticism from the floor of the Congress was also one of the factors which contributed to the decline of his personal popularity from around this time [54: *193*].

It is tempting to conclude that both before and after 1989, Gorbachev was able to use his position to act independently of both liberals and conservatives, but this is one of the most contentious issues surrounding Gorbachev. Service argues that, as long as Yeltsin was in the Politburo, Gorbachev 'found it useful to play off Yeltsin and Ligachev against each other' [11: 452], freeing Gorbachev from the influence of either. Suny, however, sees the inconsistencies of Gorbachev's rule as a result of the competing pressures of the two wings: 'He wavered back and forth, from left to right ...' [12: 457]. There is good reason to suppose that at different times, both wings were able to exert sufficient pressure to either block or accelerate the reform programme. At the beginning of 1987, the conservatives, with the weight of the party machinery behind them, seemed to be in the ascendancy. Gorbachev's attempt to have committee secretaries within the Party elected by secret ballot failed in January, while opposition to proposed reform measures meant that a planned session of the CC had to be postponed three times [5: 106–7]. The aftermath of the Andreeva letter and the results of the March 1989 elections seemed to swing the pendulum the other way. The Inter-Regional Group, while always a relatively small minority in the Congress, was not without influence. A symbolically key aim of the group, and of Andrei Sakharov, was to obtain the reformulation of Article Six of the Soviet Constitution, which guaranteed the leading role of the Communist Party. In a poignant twist, it was on the crest of the wave of sympathy and respect which followed Sakharov's death in December 1989 that this aim was finally achieved. Late in 1990 there appeared to be another shift back to the Right, as Gorbachev responded to the emergence of popular opposition forces by demoting leading reformers and promoting conservatives in their place, culminating in the resignation of Eduard Shevardnadze from the Foreign Ministry with the remark that the personnel reshuffles amounted to a 'crawling coup' [42: 55]. Gorbachev joked with journalists that he was not moving to the Right but 'going round in circles' [7: 203]. By this time, however, who Gorbachev was promoting and demoting mattered less than what was happening more broadly in the country as a whole.

It is also not entirely clear that Gorbachev was always attempting some sort of balancing act, rather than throwing in his lot with one side or the other. This is what he appeared to do in March 1988 when he met in a *dacha* (weekend cottage) outside Moscow with a group of reformers including Yakovlev, Lukianov, Shakhnazarov and Chernaev to discuss proposals for *demokratizatsiia*, forming what Strayer describes as 'Gorbachev and his inner circle, a minority even within the leadership' [5: *108*]. But whatever his intentions, Gorbachev could never have been entirely free to pursue his own programme while ignoring the views of those around him. If initially the reform programme was blocked by the dominant conservatism of the CPSU, the removal of this obstacle opened up new dangers. On the one hand, there was the fear that, as *glasnost* proceeded, the radical reformers would be capable of mobilising support in broader sections of society. On the other hand, Gorbachev was well aware of what had befallen Nikita Khrushchev in 1964 and in the background, whatever happened to the CPSU, there were the armed forces, the KGB and the MVD who might seek to impose their own solution to the Soviet Union's problems. In the event, both fears were realised: the former in the street demonstrations, strikes and national movements which grew in frequency from 1989 onwards, and the latter in the failed coup attempt of August 1991. Both issues are discussed further in Part Three.

For the time being, *demokratizatsiia*, whatever its intentions, had struck a blow against the conservatives while at the same time accommodating the radical liberals as a vocal but ineffective minority. In seeking to open up politics Gorbachev had, at the official level, neutered it. With the Communist Party now an impotent and divided force, what form of political rule would fill the vacuum? According to McCauley, the election of Gorbachev as President of the Soviet Union by the Congress of People's Deputies on 15 March 1990 filled the vacuum by instituting a period of presidential rule (what McCauley calls 'Perestroika Mark III') [56: *164–6, 264*]. But Suny identifies a completely different consequence to what he sees as the undermining of the role of the Communist Party in 1989: 'From that moment on, power flowed away from the party and its leader, into the streets, the national republics, and the meeting rooms of independent political and social organisations' [12: *468*]. Either way, the election and meeting of the first Congress of People's Deputies in the early summer of 1989 opened a new, and final, era in Soviet politics which is the subject of the last part of this book.

12 National Conflicts and Popular Fronts

The national unrest in Yakutia and Kazakhstan in 1986 (Chapter 9) turned out to be just a taste of what was to come. In the first years of *glasnost*, activists in a number of the republics on the borderlands of the Soviet Union started to campaign over local environmental threats such as those posed by nuclear power, construction of a hydroelectric dam and pollution by a phosphate plant in the Baltic republics of Estonia, Latvia and Lithuania, erosion of agricultural land in Central Asia, and nuclear waste, pollution from a rubber factory, and the long-term pollution to Lake Sevan in Armenia. The focal points of the environmental movements in the non-Russian republics resulted from a geographical coincidence (although one which was brought about partly by design) which saw many of the most polluting and environmentally damaging industries located on the peripheries of the Soviet Union. But the movements were also reflections of the greater readiness to protest of some non-Russians, who had been less willing to see themselves as a part of the Soviet system or the Communist world. In addition, local leaders were already feeling both the benefits and the threats posed by the loosening of central control, and were unwilling to intervene against such movements. National protest was not altogether confined to the Republics, as from the summer of 1987 Crimean Tatars, who had been deported wholesale from their

73

homeland by Stalin in 1944, and Jews took their protests onto the streets of Moscow.

In Armenia, mounting protests soon took a sharp turn in a different direction. The second half of 1987 saw a growing, and at first peaceful, campaign to unite Nagorno–Karabakh, an autonomous region within the Azerbaijan SSR, populated largely by Armenians, with the Armenian SSR. By the end of the year violence broke out on a small scale in the village of Chardakhly to the north-west of Karabakh when Armenian demonstrators were assaulted. In February 1988 mass demonstrations of up to 250,000 people were organised in the Armenian capital Erevan over the issue. On 20 February the Karabakh regional Soviet organised an unofficial referendum, obtaining 80,000 signatures in favour of uniting with Armenia. Shortly afterwards, more serious conflict broke out between Armenians and Azeris near Askeran, leaving 50 Armenians wounded and two Azeris dead. This incident was the prelude to the massacre of Armenians in the Azeri town of Sumgait which took at least 32 lives. In the following months unrest took the form of strikes and demonstrations, and thousands of Azeris living in Armenia and Armenians living in Azerbaijan fled across the border. In November, tens of thousands of Azeri demonstrators set up camp in Lenin Square in Baku (the capital of the Azerbaijan SSR), leading the republic to declare a state of emergency. The Armenian SSR declared that Nagorno–Karabakh would now be under its control, and the Soviet government's response was to declare temporary direct rule from Moscow over the disputed region, a solution which only served to inflame the situation. Further ethnic bloodshed broke out in Baku on 13–14 January 1990 and spread to other areas. On the night of 20 January Soviet Red Army troops entered Baku to restore order, leaving over 120 civilian dead and more than 700 wounded (at least according to an investigation by the independent commission 'Shield' – the Soviets admitted to much smaller losses) [27: 216]. As the Soviet Union eventually fell apart in 1991, the dispute developed into all-out war between the two newly independent republics.

Further ethnic conflicts erupted involving Abkhaz and Ossetian minorities in Georgia in 1989, between Kirgiz and Uzbeks in the Osh region of Kirgizia in 1990 and, after the collapse of the Soviet Union, between Ossetians and Ingush in the North Caucasus region of the Russian Federation in 1992. Much of the western literature on these conflicts, particularly those between Armenians and Azeris, focuses on the issue of blame and is often highly partisan, mostly in favour of the Armenians [85]. Audrey Altstadt provides a more balanced view of the conflict, highlighting the role of both Armenian and Azeri elites in stoking and prolonging the violence [27: *195–219*]. The role of local government elites in provoking conflict in Georgia is also highlighted by Stephen Jones, who blames the 'single-minded pursuit of Georgianisation' by the Gamsakhurdia government [78: *512–13*].

While *glasnost* provoked violence between different national groups in many southern regions of the USSR, national movements in the Baltic region and in Georgia proved much more of a direct threat to the Soviet system. In Estonia, Latvia and Lithuania, memories of the Soviet annexations in 1939 and 1945 were still very much alive, and the Soviets were still widely viewed as an occupying and Russifying force. High levels of education and a more developed economy than the Soviet average contributed to the sense of hostile foreign colonialism. Mass national organisations known as Popular Fronts were formed in all three republics between April and October 1988, and rapidly began to mobilise the population and to put pressure on newly appointed governments. Demands for republican sovereignty, new language laws, and the readopting of traditional national symbols soon escalated into calls for outright independence. In August 1989, on the 50th anniversary of the Molotov–Ribbentrop pact which had sealed the fate of the previously independent republics by agreement between the Soviet Union and Nazi Germany, over a million Estonians, Latvians and Lithuanians joined hands in a human chain which stretched across all three republics. By the end of the year, under pressure from the mass movement, all three republics had declared the illegality of their incorporation into the Soviet Union in 1940 – effectively a declaration of intent to pursue independence. The Popular Fronts were overwhelmingly victorious in free elections, and independence was initially declared in Lithuania on 11 March 1990, in Estonia on 30 March and Latvia on 4 May.

A popular movement for independence on a comparable scale emerged at the same time in Georgia, where a series of mass demonstrations in support of independence eventually provoked a violent response from the Red Army, which killed 19 demonstrators at a rally in the capital Tbilisi in April 1989. Elsewhere the national movement was less powerful and, as already mentioned, a referendum in March 1991 indicated support for maintaining the Soviet Union in the remaining republics. Declarations of sovereignty by republican governments, new laws on language and on other cultural matters went unopposed by Moscow, and Gorbachev's willingness to negotiate a new, looser, Union treaty, appeared for a while to be sufficient for a majority of the republics to ensure their continued adherence to the Union. By that time, however, further impetus had been added to the centrifugal forces of the Soviet Union from an unexpected source – the RSFSR or, as it was known by then, the Russian Federation. Shortly after he was elected chairman of the Supreme Soviet of the RSFSR in March 1990, Boris Yeltsin made plain to the Baltic republics that he would not stand in the way of their secession from the USSR and even called on the minorities in the autonomous republics and regions of his own republic to 'take whatever helping of power that you can gobble up'. As the communist system finally unravelled in the wake of the August 1991 coup, it was Yeltsin who took the lead in opposing Gorbachev's plans for a new Union Treaty and promoting a looser Commonwealth of Independent States instead. Yeltsin's motives for taking Russia in this direction is discussed in Chapter 16. A second referendum in Ukraine, on 1 December 1991, which now showed overwhelming support for independence, dealt the final blow to Gorbachev's plans [80: *64*]. This apparent about-turn in public opinion in the USSR's second largest republic illustrates the volatility of national sentiment (although confusion over the terms of Gorbachev's March referendum may have exaggerated the extent of the about-turn in public opinion) [35].

Thus the breakup of the USSR into 15 separate republics accompanied the collapse of the communist system. For all the violence and the mass demonstrations in the Baltic and Transcaucasian republics, in retrospect this might still seem a surprising outcome given the relative weakness of similar movements in the largest non-Russian republics, Ukraine and Belarus, and the republics of Central Asia inhabited largely by Muslims. Studies of the national independence movements in the Baltic Republics highlight the role of the living and collective historical memories of independence in 1918–39, the perceived economic benefits of independence, and the issue of cultural self-preservation [83: *132–4*]. The first two factors were unique to the Baltics – the rest of the Soviet Union (apart from Moldavia) had been a part of the Russian Empire since at least the middle of the nineteenth century and only enjoyed brief independence in the course of 1918–21, while the southern republics probably benefited overall from the net Soviet economic investment. The third factor suggests a degree of cultural–national mobilisation which was evident in Georgia but not elsewhere. This raises the possibility that, while democracy was ultimately incompatible with the Baltic republics and, perhaps, Georgia, for the remaining part of the Soviet Union, there was no good reason for the other republics to leave. Thus the explanation has been advanced that this was really an accident – Ukraine and so on were influenced by a sort of domino effect which inspired them to follow the Baltic example [75: *11*]. For a number of years following the breakup of the Soviet Union, the idea that it had been a mistake gained certain credibility as economic crisis, authoritarianism, and internal conflicts swept across a number of the independent republics, while Belarus, in particular, sought to reforge links with Russia.

Valeriy Tishkov, a Russian academic who was later to serve for a while as Boris Yeltsin's Minister for Nationalities in post-Soviet Russia, explains the collapse largely in terms of the motives of political elites within the republics. Under the Soviet system, while they were able to wield considerable power in their own republics, they were unable to enjoy the trappings of that power and the wealth and privilege that they might attain as leaders of an independent state. Tishkov argues that the Soviet Union might have stayed together as a geographical entity if only Gorbachev had paid more attention to the privileges of the republican leaders, citing his own later observation to Gorbachev personally that: 'he should have abolished *Vyezdnaya komissia* (a special Department of the Communist Party's CC which granted permission for trips abroad) and should have allowed republican leaders to have personal jets for business flights' [35: *44*]. Other interpretations combine elite motivation with popular aspirations. Ben Fowkes' study also assigns a major role to republican elites, but combines this with the growth of pressures from below under the impact of *glasnost* and the collapse of central authority. Thus, 'the greatest role in the disintegration of the Soviet Union was played by Gorbachev himself' [28: *196*].

The sudden and largely unanticipated upsurge in popular nationalism is explained in a sophisticated analysis by Ronald Suny as not only a direct product of *glasnost*, but as resulting from a peculiarity of the Soviet situation. The Soviet regime, through the official ideology of Marxism–Leninism, had claimed to be building a classless regime and had, therefore, appropriated the language of class struggle to its own uses. As economic decline set in and accelerated, reaction to the subsequent fall in living standards could therefore not possibly be expressed in class terms, leading citizens to adopt the only other form of personal identity open to them – that of the nation [34: *120–4*]. Thus the strength of the national movement and the weakness of the labour movement were two sides of the same coin. In social and economic terms, in most of the republics few people stood to benefit from the collapse and its occurrence was therefore far from inevitable. It took a combination of the consolidation of national identities promoted by the Soviet system with a series of contingent factors associated with Gorbachev's policies and economic decline for the collapse to occur as and when it did [31: *159–60*].

The national breakup of the Soviet Union is one of the areas where historians are divided as to whether a short- or a long-term perspective needs to be taken. Most of the interpretations advanced above stress the role of recent developments, albeit in the context of the longer term impact of Soviet nationalities policies. At the other extreme is the argument that the Soviet Union, forcibly created out of the ruins of the Russian Empire by Lenin's Red Army, effectively used repression and Russification to put a lid on the burgeoning national movements of the early twentieth century, which were to reemerge in full force as soon as Gorbachev's *glasnost* took the pressure off. A growing consensus among historians that, with some exceptions, national identities were weak before the Russian Revolution and that it was Soviet policies that strengthened them, undermines a part of this argument [30]. Still, historian Richard Pipes maintains that ultimately the triumph of nationalism is inevitable: 'ethnic and territorial loyalties, when in conflict with class allegiances, everywhere and at all times overwhelm them, dissolving Communism in nationalism ...' [4: *155*]. A slightly different argument, based on comparative studies, is that all empires have a limited lifespan and are ultimately bound to be undone by the force of their inner contradictions, a case most forcefully made by Alexander Motyl [81]. Motyl's argument, however, has been criticised for deducing generalisations that were not entirely valid, for ignoring the specific circumstances of the Soviet collapse, and for assuming that the breakup of the 'Empire' precipitated the collapse of communism, rather than the other way around [84: 5, 86: 92].

The sudden and, to most commentators, surprising explosion of national unrest in the late 1980s, does not in itself prove that the division of the USSR along national lines was an inevitable event waiting to happen. For most of the Soviet period, nationality policies were successful in integrating diverse peoples under a single state. The policy did contain its own contradictions – promoting ethnic particularism at the same time as denying the relevance of those differences and clearly giving first preference to the Russians. Complacency and even deliberate encouragement of national tensions certainly provided fuel to any potential flames of national conflict. But some of these contradictions can equally be interpreted as signs of flexibility within the policy which was successful in holding the USSR together long after the world's other great empires had disintegrated. This flexibility was not, however, sufficient to adapt successfully to the totally different circumstances of the Baltic nationalities incorporated after 1945. Outside of the Baltics, it was ethnic conflict in the Caucasus which provided the strongest indications of failure of national policy. But these events are linked to economic and political upheaval as much as to any long-standing but suppressed nationalist tendencies. Recent investigations by social scientists suggest that ethnic conflict and secessionist tendencies are prone to arise in situations of uncertainty where different groups are induced to compete for perceived future advantages [77], a process which can only be reinforced by the effects noted by Suny. National unrest in turn fed into political and economic turmoil, creating a declining spiral from which the USSR received its eventual deathblows.

13 Strikes and Mass Protest

The release of Sakharov and other political prisoners at the end of the year 1986 was followed by the creation of small organisations devoted to the release of further prisoners. In addition to the mushrooming of criticism by intellectuals under the impact of *glasnost*, more informal movements arose among Soviet youth based on alternative lifestyles and focused in particular on sports and various forms of rock music. More open forms of protest began initially around local issues connected to the preservation of old buildings and the environment, and developed into larger scale environmental protests, especially in the republics [65].

Significant mass political protest emerged around the election campaign of March 1989, particularly in connection with the nomination of Boris Yeltsin to stand as a candidate in the city of Moscow, which brought thousands onto the streets. Yeltsin's ability to mobilise popular support became even more apparent when he failed to gain one of the places reserved for Moscow deputies on the Supreme Soviet chosen by the Congress of People's Deputies – more mass demonstrations followed. When a Siberian delegate offered to give up his place to Yeltsin, it allowed Gorbachev, in a move which was barely constitutional, to admit Yeltsin to the Supreme Soviet, although whether this was a result of mass protests or more of a manouevre on Gorbachev's part to co-opt Yeltsin is disputed [54: *192*]. Yeltsin and the radical reformers were by now masters of the art of mass politics, a tactic that had not been seen on any scale since the Russian Revolution. A series of protests culminating in a mass rally of a quarter of a million people on 4 February 1990 helped them secure the constitutional change which abolished the official leading role of the Communist Party of the Soviet Union.

Another form of protest which emerged on a wider scale than what had been evident since the Second World War was workers' strikes. Encouraged by the rhetoric of *glasnost*, workers resorted to strikes in cities like Iaroslavl and Leningrad over wages, hours and conditions, but rarely raised political demands. From small beginnings in 1987, workers began to form their own associations, first at a local level and often during a strike or immediately after one. These groups began to make contact with each other and in February 1988, a movement called the Club for the Democratisation of Trade Unions was formed with the aim of revitalising the official Party-run trade unions. In 1989, the first new independent trade unions appeared, and by 1991 there existed a number of competing trade union federations, like the Union of Socialist Trade Unions (*Sotsprof*) and the Federation of Independent Trade Unions of the RSFSR (FNPR).

The most significant strikes were carried out by miners. In July 1989, a strike in the western Siberian coalfields spread to the Kuzbass, Vorkuta and Komi in the north and the Donbass in Ukraine. At its peak half a million workers were on strike in every major coalfield in the Soviet Union. The strikes were mostly in response to shortages created by the severe economic crisis, and the principal demands were for higher wages and pensions, improved working conditions and the abolition of compulsory work on Sundays. But strikers also called for the relaxation of central control of the coal industry and the right for work collectives to sell coal produced above the planned targets – demands which, while in themselves addressing the miners' economic conditions, challenged the whole political and economic principles of the Soviet system. The miners also refused to return to work until they had met with senior political figures. By the time Vorkuta miners struck again in October 1989, their demands were more overtly political. They demanded the recognition of independent workers' organisations and protested against a recent Supreme Soviet law banning strikes in key industries. They also gave their support to the campaign to amend Article 6 of the Soviet constitution, which guaranteed the leading role of the CPSU. A widely observed one-day miners' strike on 11 July 1990 was directly political in its demands. In March 1991 a strike by miners in the Donbass, initially over wage levels, spread to the Kuzbass and Vorkuta fields and eventually to other industries. This time the strikers demanded the resignation of Gorbachev and the dissolution of the Congress of People's Deputies. Inspite of a large number of economic conces- sions being offered, the strikes did not die down until Yeltsin himself called for an end after he had reached an agreement with Gorbachev and the other republics over the future constitutional structure of the USSR on 23 April [62].

It has already been noted in Chapter 10 that authors such as McCauley and Suny deny that the introduction of *demokratizatsiia* was the result of any pressures from below. This is not to say that they ignore the influence of mass politics, especially during and after the 1989 elections. McCauley highlights the role of mass demonstrations in providing the legitimacy of popular support to Yeltsin's Inter-Regional Group [56: *111*]. Suny goes as far as referring to them as a 'revolution from below' [12: *468*]. Robert Service underplays the ability of strikes and other forms of protest to influ- ence Gorbachev's reform programme: 'the Soviet authorities weathered the storm. The strikers lived in far-flung areas, and Ryzhkov and his fellow ministers managed to isolate them from the rest of society by quickly offering higher wages' [11: *472*].

Others are less dismissive. Mike Haynes cites Gorbachev's reaction to the 1989 strikes as evidence of the seriousness with which they were taken: the strike, Gorbachev said, was the 'worst ordeal to befall our country in all the four years of restructuring'. The strikes had an empowering effect on the miners and showed glimpses of an alternative future, giving them 'an element of that self-respect, dignity and confidence that must be the basis of any real alternative either to the system as it was then or the system as it would become' [7: *187–8*]. That potential, Haynes argues, was not fulfilled as a result of the historical, ideological and organisational factors that weakened the workers' movement. Instead, the immediate conse- quences were negative – the strikes frightened off those of Yeltsin's radical supporters who had seen the possibility of an alliance with workers as a way of pushing ahead the reform programme, while it gave Gorbachev the pretext to introduce anti-strike legislation and pushed liberal reformers like Anatolii Sobchak in a more conserv- ative direction [7: *200–1*].

Jonathan Aves gives a far more prominent place to the workers' movement in determining the fate of Soviet communism: 'The strikes of March–April 1991 were the nearest that the new Russian labour movement came to playing the role of a Russian Solidarnosc and it played a crucial role in breaking Gorbachev's half-hearted attempt to halt the process of reform and in putting the Soviet Union on the road to the August coup and its final break-up' [62: *153*]. While recognising the long-term weakness of the movement, Aves' argument is based on the conjuncture of the 1991 strikes with a crucial moment in the struggle between conservatives and reformers, giving Yeltsin a decisive edge, and in the evolving relationship between the republics. Any argument that workers brought down the system, then, rests on their indirect influence, not on any characterisation of a revolution from below.

Donald Filtzer's study of the labour process under *perestroika* sees the role of the working class not so much in what it did do, as in what it did not do. For him, the key dilemma faced by Gorbachev and the reformers was that in order to improve the performance of the Soviet economy, the labour process needed to be restructured in a way that 'would require a frontal assault on the network of defensive practices which workers had developed over decades as a way to insulate themselves ... from the exploitation and repression of the Stalinist system'. Securing worker participation in this process would require a rise in standards of living which was impossible in the current economic circumstances. Thus the regime was caught in a vicious circle, unable to carry out the labour reforms which were necessary to save the economy precisely because the economy was in such a bad shape. Strikes and other protests which did occur were sufficient to remind enterprise managers and politicians alike of the dangers of a confrontation with the workforce. The mere threat of strike action was enough, then, at the local level to win concessions, and at the more general level to scare the regime off from pushing through unpopular economic and workplace reforms [64: *214–17*].

From the earliest days of the Soviet Union, its leaders were not blind to the irony that working class unrest against the workers' state undermined any semblance of legitimacy enjoyed by the regime. In contrast to the national unrest, which the regime was prepared to tolerate and even encourage within certain limits, and to the dreadful treatment of the peasantry by successive leaders, workers were treated with much more caution. Compared to western societies, skilled workers in particular enjoyed, relative to middle-class professionals, a privileged position [67: *155–60*]. When unrest did occur, it was met instantly either with brutal repression, as in Novocherkassk in 1962 [14] (or Budapest in 1956), or with immediate satisfaction of strikers' demands, and was thus contained within individual localities.

These traditions underpinned the desperate attempts of Gorbachev, Ryzhkov and Yeltsin to win over or at least neutralise this constituency. Miners, although working in difficult and dangerous conditions, were in other respects the most privileged of all workers [67: *157*]. But it was this very fact which made them the most likely to react against the inevitable privations caused by economic decline. Although, at the time, many on the western left looked to the working class movement to provide an alternative for the future of the USSR and its republics [40], in retrospect this appears to have been too big a task. Shorn of any organisational independence, workers were deterred for obvious reasons from looking to the set of ideas and organisational principles most likely to answer their needs – socialism – which had been so thoroughly expropriated and discredited by the regime. The liberals who sought to co-opt the workers' movement naturally recoiled from encouraging strikes beyond a certain point. Those radicals among the younger generation who might have considered an alternative found the weight of the past and the current state of politics too great a barrier to overcome.

14 Repression and Resistance

The initial response to *glasnost* was cautious and controlled. Initially, it was confined to debates over Soviet history and intellectual discourse on a range of themes from immediate economic reform to literature and was conducted in journals and newspapers which were easily subjected to containment through close central control. We have seen in the previous two chapters how, from tentative and nervous beginnings, different groups in society gradually engaged themselves in more and more open protest. But *glasnost* did not mean that freedom of speech and political activity was installed overnight. Such liberties were, after all, unheard of in over 1000 years of Russian history, with brief exceptions in the revolutionary years of 1905 and 1917. The KGB and MVD kept up their surveillance and harassment of dissidents. The party *nomenklatura* system ensured, until democracy took over, that political careers could be abruptly halted for anyone who stepped out of line, and Gorbachev in the early years of his rule did not hesitate to use his powers of appointment to stifle political opponents. Even as late as 1988 just attempting to set up a political party was a cause for arrest.

A number of incidents suggested that the ruling party, the military and the police might never abandon their long-trusted methods of control. Police charges against Tatar demonstrators in Moscow in July 1987, and the shooting of demonstrators in Tbilisi in April 1989 aroused international condemnation as well as that of Soviet liberals. In January 1990 MVD troops were mobilised to deal with the mass demonstrations in Moscow, although on this occasion conflict was avoided. The Soviet state and Gorbachev did not cover themselves with glory in their handling of ethnic violence either. The Red

Army's occupation of Baku in January 1990 was not only a direct cause of bloodshed in itself, it came too late to prevent the intercommunal violence over the Karabakh question. According to Audrey Altstadt the claim that Soviet troops were needed to protect innocent civilians was only a cover for Gorbachev's real motives: 'Gorbachev sent troops to Baku to shore up communist power there, justifying that act with a barrage of excuses, playing on internal Soviet and western misinformation and fears of a resurgent Islam. Despite his rhetoric, he acted like a Russian imperial leader preserving power in a colony.' Altstadt comments that Gorbachev was able to get away with this in Azerbaijan only because the West, occupied at that time with a war against Saddam Hussein in the Gulf, was not interested [27: *217*].

The negligence displayed by the West towards events in the Caucasus was emphasised by the far greater attention paid to an event that was much less costly in terms of lives, but was closer to the western media's centre of attention, in Lithuania. The events there of 11–12 January 1991 presented the greatest challenge yet to Gorbachev's democratic credentials. In 1989 and 1990 Lithuania became the main battleground for his efforts to hold the Soviet Union together. The Lithuanian Supreme Soviet led the way in declaring the republic's sovereignty on 18 May 1989, and in declaring the 1940 incorporation into the USSR illegal. On 6 December, the same body declared an end to the CPSU's political monopoly and legalised opposition parties. The prospect of Lithuania finally breaking away from the USSR emerged as a real possibility with the electoral triumph of the nationalist Sajudis party in February 1990. Gorbachev's response wavered between concessions, like the July 1989 sanctioning of free market reforms in the republic, through persuasion, demonstrated by a personal visit to Vilnius to hold talks with communist leaders in January 1990, and to outright threats, like the decree ordering all firearms in Lithuania to be handed in to the Soviet Union's Ministry of Internal Affairs in March 1990. Force was applied later the same month when paratroopers took over the headquarters of the Lithuanian Communist Party and went on to detain Lithuanian army deserters at a Vilnius hospital. Roughly around the same time, Gorbachev called for the annulment of Lithuania's declaration of independence. A meeting between the Lithuanian government and Gorbachev in October did little to ease the tension, and was followed by a propaganda campaign in which Lithuania was accused of drawing up lists of communists to be executed and of planning to annex territory from neighbouring republics [56: *198*].

On 7 January 1991, Soviet paratroopers entered all three Baltic republics, and were greeted by thousands of Russian demonstrators, who proceeded to break into the Lithuanian Supreme Council building. In response to a call from the Sajudis leader Vitautas Landsbergis, Lithuanians rushed to protect the parliament, and forced the resignation of the pro-Gorbachev Prime Minister Kazimiera Prunskiene. Gorbachev demanded the full restoration of the constitution of the USSR in the republic and, before there was time for any response, on 11 January troops began to occupy the airport and to move into other parts of the city, firing at demonstrators along the way. About 5000 protestors formed a ring around the television station, which now became the focus of conflict. On the afternoon of 12 January, troops stormed the TV tower, leaving 13 dead and 165 injured in their wake.

On this occasion there were no excuses, as there had been in Baku, about protecting civilians from each other. The issue was the sovereignty and independence of Lithuania from the USSR. Both at the time and ever since the question of Gorbachev's responsibility for the military action has been disputed. He himself has always denied giving the order, but so has everybody else, and Landsbergis has claimed that he tried in vain to contact Gorbachev over two days in order to try and find a peaceful solution to the crisis. But whether or not Gorbachev gave the orders, the incident tarnished his reputation at home and abroad. To the minds of many, Gorbachev's willingness to use force in order to preserve the unity of the USSR or to intimidate political opponents was evidence of the the provisional nature of his commitment to democracy. The view that state violence and authoritarianism were endemic in Russian history and culture appeared to be confirmed later when Boris Yeltsin, the hero of democracy in 1991, sent troops against the Russian parliament in 1993 and invaded the breakaway republic of Chechnya in 1994.

This fits with the view that *glasnost* and *demokratizatsiia* were tactics employed by Gorbachev in order to secure the pursuit of a series of reforms whose ultimate aim was to preserve the Soviet communist system. But Gorbachev had developed politically in the Brezhnev years and when push came to shove, he would not shrink from resorting to the tried and tested methods. On such a view it was largely down to the obvious strength of the popular movement by

1990, when *glasnost* had already gone too far, that he did not risk further repressive measures which might have plunged the country into civil war, while the bungled coup of August 1991 meant he could no longer rely even on military commanders should he seek to preserve communism by force. But from another perspective, the picture looks quite different. Outside of Transcaucasia, the collapse and breakup of one of the most powerful and authoritarian states of the twentieth century was accompanied by remarkably little bloodshed. Street demonstrations were mostly allowed to proceed without hindrance, while the typical response to strikes was to negotiate and offer concessions. Robert Strayer considers Gorbachev's personal values to have played a major role in preventing bloodshed: 'Gorbachev … deserves considerable credit for his country's peaceful demise. His unwillingness to countenance large-scale violence, his desire to humanize and democratize Soviet socialism and make it consonant with western values … all served to delegitimize the use of force as the basis for political order' [5: *199–200*]. Suraska is another who emphasises Gorbachev's personal distaste for any form of violence in the pursuit of political ends [42: *32*].

Gorbachev had invested heavily in mobilising the support of his own population and of international opinion behind his reform programme. To resort to violence against opponents of any sort would threaten to undermine all these efforts. In addition to the traditional wariness of provoking or escalating workers' unrest discussed in Chapter 13, Russian and Soviet leaders were particularly aware of the possibility of disobedience in the armed forces who, after all, had played a key role in overthrowing both the Tsar and the Provisional Government in 1917. Also, even if military intervention passed off without these fears being realised, its use would increase the influence of the army commanders who were not, perhaps, Gorbachev's most natural supporters. As it turns out, the events of August 1991 underlined the reluctance of the military to involve itself in politics at the time. One explanation for this reluctance is the traditional rivalry between the military and the KGB, seen as being behind the coup, and the depoliticisation of the armed forces as a direct result of Gorbachev's policies [42: *57–82*]. These considerations, quite apart from any natural humanistic or moral objections on Gorbachev's part, meant that the resort to large-scale repression in defence of his own power or of the Soviet system was not a realistic option.

15 The International Impact

The most pressing issue facing the Soviet military in 1985 was that of the intervention in Afghanistan, launched in 1979. It soon became clear that the duration and scale of this intervention would be much greater than anticipated. The war in Afghanistan was not only a drain on manpower and finances, it was turning into a national humiliation comparable with the earlier US involvement in Vietnam. Those young soldiers who survived were often returning to the Soviet Union in a state of severe trauma and addicted to the drugs that were readily available in the conflict zones. The deeper *glasnost* progressed, the harder it was to cover up or ignore the impact of the war. Gorbachev's initial response was to escalate the military offensive, although this may have been a temporary measure aimed at better positioning of the Soviet Union in any future negotiations over withdrawal [36: 727]. The announcement of Soviet withdrawal in January 1988 was ratified at a summit with the USA in Geneva in April. The removal of at least regular forces was completed in 1989, thus drawing the curtain over one of the more shameful episodes in the history of the Soviet military, but not without leaving a bitter legacy behind.

The withdrawal from Afghanistan was one part of a much broader reappraisal of Soviet foreign policy which radically transformed international relations and brought an end to the Cold War. Up to 25 per cent of the Soviet economy may have been devoted to the military, spurred on mostly by the Arms Race with the USA. One interpretation of Gorbachev's foreign policy therefore is to link it to a desperate attempt to save the Soviet economy from bankruptcy, as many of the more cynical observers believed at the time. However, most later commentators are agreed that genuine principles underlay what became known as Gorbachev's 'New Thinking', based on humanitarian principles coupled with a reconceptualisation of the Soviet national interest.

The term 'New Thinking' was employed by Gorbachev even before he became General Secretary. In a speech to the British Parliament on 18 December 1984, Gorbachev outlined some key elements of his future foreign policy: East and West should look for the common ground between them rather than those factors which created distance, and should learn to recognise each other's legitimate interests and be prepared to make compromises. He also emphasised that the Soviet Union itself needed international peace in order to successfully pursue a changing domestic agenda. It was in connection with this same visit to the UK that Prime Minister Margaret Thatcher made her famous statement: 'I like Mr. Gorbachev. We can do business together', which itself testifies to the extent to which Gorbachev represented a departure from earlier Soviet leaders in international negotiations.

'New Thinking' has been summarised as resting on three linked doctrinal developments: (1) Competing class or national interests were no longer the principle factor in world politics. Instead, the interdependence and mutual concerns of all the major states dominated the international system; (2) Warfare was not an acceptable way of resolving conflicts of interest; (3) Competition between the Communist East and Capitalist West was no longer the main axis of world politics – the Cold War was over [37: 290–6]. Underpinning the New Thinking was a recognition of the scale of global threats to both East and West – in particular, the possibility of nuclear war, but also the threat of ecological disaster and instability caused by global poverty (international terrorism was another area of mutual interest, but to nowhere near the extent it was to become in later decades). Abandoning the traditional Soviet confrontational attitude also meant a radical rethinking of military doctrine. If it was recognised that ultimately neither side could be victorious in a nuclear war, there was little sense in planning for an offensive war. Even conventional warfare in Europe was rejected as being potentially too destructive to achieve any real benefits for the victor. The new emphasis was on 'reasonable defensive sufficiency' – ensuring that the Soviet Union would be able to fight a defensive war while simultaneously conducting negotiations to bring hostilities to an end.

Periods of détente and efforts to co-operate with Western powers had been characteristic of earlier Soviet foreign policy, but the doctrinal shift represented by New Thinking was immense. Gorbachev showed his hand as a radical in international relations sooner and more openly than was the case in domestic policy. The key aim of the new policy, which simultaneously offered some relief to the crippling problems of the Soviet budget, was partial or total nuclear disarmament. As early as 7 April 1985, Gorbachev declared a unilateral moratorium on the further deployment of intermediate range SS-20 missiles in Europe. At his first meeting with US President Ronald Reagan in Geneva in November 1985, the traditional tone of East–West summits was immediately broken when what was supposed to be a 15-minute informal introduction turned into a 'Fireside Summit' between the two, with only interpreters present, and which lasted over an hour. Gorbachev offered an immediate mutual reduction in long-range nuclear weapons by 50 per cent. Although Reagan responded positively to this initiative, a sticking point was the US Strategic Defence Initiative (SDI) – the so-called 'Star Wars' programme of anti-missile systems orbiting in space. In January 1986, Gorbachev announced a three-stage programme towards complete nuclear disarmament, and by the end of the year a concrete step had been taken at the CSCE Conference on Confidence and Security-Building Measures in Stockholm on 22 September. While the agreements resulting from this conference concerned notification and observation of military exercises rather than disarmament itself, Soviet concessions regarding on-site missile inspections represented a considerable departure from traditional secrecy and set the ground for more substantive talks at Reykjavik in October.

At the US-Soviet summit in Reykjavik, Gorbachev suggested a total removal of SS-20s from Europe and a halving of long-range missiles. Whether Reagan and his negotiators were simply unprepared for such an offer, or were too suspicious of Soviet motives and unwilling to abandon SDI for domestic political reasons, Gorbachev's move was not reciprocated. Negotiations for real arms reductions moved slowly, but on a visit to Washington in December 1987 the Intermediate Nuclear Forces treaty was signed. The new tone in Soviet-US relations was symbolised by reciprocal visits by Reagan and Gorbachev to each other's countries in 1988 and, in one of his last acts as an international statesman, Gorbachev signed the far-reaching Strategic Arms Reduction Treaty (START) with Reagan's successor George Bush snr in Moscow in July 1991.

Throughout these negotiations, Gorbachev was vulnerable to the charge that he was selling out Soviet defence interests and opening the way for US global domination through a series of unilateral concessions which the USA was not prepared to match. The appearance that the Soviet Union was either declaring a series of one-sided reductions or acceding on each occasion to maximal US demands was not helped by the continuing belligerence of the USA, illustrated in particular by the invasion of Panama in 1989 and intervention in Kuwait in 1990–91. These actions and the initial reluctance to accede to Soviet offers of mutual disarmament undermined Gorbachev's claim to be leading the world into a new era in which recognition of mutual interests would replace aggressive impulses [55: 85]. As a result, Gorbachev's international policies were a cause of concern not just for the Soviet military, but for broader sections of the population. On the other hand, however slow the actual progress of disarmament, Gorbachev could claim with some justification to have transformed the whole tenor of international relations by bringing the USA to the negotiating table and from a position of moral advantage, bringing an end to the Cold War and focusing great power politics on problem-solving rather than confrontation [37: 320–1].

Just how far Gorbachev was prepared to go in pursuit of a new foreign policy agenda was brought home by events in Eastern Europe in 1989. The other communist regimes were under pressures similar to those at work in the Soviet Union in favour of reform, and ultimately the end of the communist regimes was a result of internal forces. But whereas in the past (in Hungary in 1956 and Czechoslovakia in 1968, most recently in Poland in 1980–81 when General Jaruzelski's imposition of martial law owed much to Soviet pressure) the Soviet Union had always insisted on its satellite states remaining within certain limits, and had been ready to preserve communism by force; now Gorbachev not only withdrew the threat of military intervention but positively encouraged reformers and oppositionists to put pressure on Brezhnev-like leaders such as East Germany's Erich Honecker. In July 1989, when events in Poland and Hungary already revealed that the fall of their communist governments might be imminent, Gorbachev explicitly rejected the so-called 'Brezhnev doctrine' by declaring that the use of military force was unthinkable 'by one alliance against another, within an alliance, or whatever it might be'. One by one, communist regimes collapsed or were toppled in Poland, Hungary, Czechoslovakia, East Germany, Bulgaria and Romania, so that by the end of 1989 the Soviet Union had lost altogether its direct sphere of influence, and could count on little or no real support from the other surviving communist regimes in Yugoslavia, Albania, China and Cuba.

Once again, Gorbachev's motives in allowing such a sudden loss of international influence can be ascribed to a combination of idealistic and practical factors. Maintaining an indirect form of Empire did not fit easily with the New Thinking, and the refusal of many of the old guard of communist leaders to contemplate the kind of reform programme Gorbachev was implementing in the USSR may have left little option but to abandon them. At the same time, the continued military presence in Eastern Europe was an additional burden on the Soviet budget and was harder to justify in military terms once the doctrine of a winnable war in Europe was abandoned. The removal of the Iron Curtain as a barrier to co-operation with Western Europe had already become a declared aim of Soviet policy [37: 306–9]. By abandoning whatever advantages might be incurred by maintaining direct influence in Eastern Europe, Gorbachev was simultaneously allowing himself more room for reform in domestic affairs, and seeking to win the backing of the western powers.

The extent to which Gorbachev himself may have been influenced by West European social-democratic ideas is a topic of some debate [55: 26–7]. But whether he was acting primarily out of ideological commitment or from a realist foreign policy commitment, his efforts to promote nuclear disarmament and disengage from the Cold War won him many friends on both the Left and the Right Wings in the West, to the extent that he was awarded the Nobel Peace Prize in 1990. However, such admiration rarely transformed into the concrete support he may have expected. When, in 1990 and 1991, Soviet and Russian leaders appealed to the G7 group of leading industrial nations, the International Monetary Fund and the World Bank for financial assistance, the response was too slow and too inadequate to provide any respite from the dire problems of the Soviet economy [22: 220, 238]. Reagan's (and later Bush's) reluctance to respond to early offers on disarmament, meant that

Gorbachev appeared to be giving away far more than he was receiving [2: *162*]. This alienated not only the Soviet military, but the broader public as well. A series of concessions made to German Chancellor Helmut Kohl over German reunification in 1990, when he was under no real pressure to make them, fuelled the feeling that Gorbachev was not acting in the Soviet Union's national interest on the international stage [42: *83–105*]. The impression that Gorbachev was busy gallivanting around the world earning the admiration of Western leaders, while the Soviet Union lost its tangible international authority and his own people slipped further into poverty, was one which conservatives and Russian nationalists could easily play on. Indeed, Gorbachev's popularity abroad may have been a major contributor to the dramatic decline of his popularity at home in 1989–91 [47: *30–1*]. Ultimately, the abandonment of the Soviet Union's role as the vanguard of international revolution and one of the world's great powers undermined yet another pillar of communist legitimacy, a loss which was not sufficiently compensated for by the economic gains resulting from the end of the Cold War.

16 The Return of Yeltsin

Yeltsin's demotion in 1987–88 appeared, to outside observers, to signal the end of his political career. But he used the opportunity of being out of the limelight to carefully nurture relations with liberal critics of Gorbachev and to position himself as their figurehead. Perhaps more importantly, the considerable popularity he had earned when in charge of both Sverdlovsk and Moscow was boosted in many quarters by his apparently principled stand. His fallout with Gorbachev and the Politburo had been conducted under the public gaze and earned him sympathy combined with admiration.

He seized the opportunity of the elections to the Congress of People's Deputies in 1989 to launch a remarkable comeback. Efforts to prevent him standing as a candidate only enhanced his image of a hero-martyr, and in securing 89 per cent of the popular vote in Moscow he gathered more personal legitimacy than any other candidate. The demonstrations surrounding this election and his effort to get a place on the Supreme Soviet marked Yeltsin out as a unique leader in his ability to mobilise popular support, and therefore a threat for Gorbachev and the conservatives to take seriously.

His continual sniping at Gorbachev in the Congress of People's Deputies further enhanced his status as the focus of liberal opposition, but for the most part, his activities were ineffective and he never looked like challenging Gorbachev as long as Soviet politics was dominated by the predominantly loyal CPSU. But in March 1990, he established an alternative basis of power by securing election to the Congress of People's Deputies of the RSFSR and then, in a narrow vote, became its chairman. Unlike in the Congress of People's Deputies of the USSR, opposition liberals were able to secure a sizeable base in the Russian equivalent, where elections were freer. The DemRossiya (Democratic Russia) movement won most of the votes in all the major cities, but fared badly in the countryside. The Congress met on 16 May, and the democrats around Yeltsin held about 40 per cent of the seats, with the conservatives holding another 40 per cent. It was therefore a bare majority of the remaining uncommitted delegates that secured Yeltsin's victory in the election for Chairman. Even then he may have owed his victory to a political mistake on the part of Gorbachev, who gave his backing to the dull, uncharismatic Aleksandr Vlasov [56: *174*].

On 12 June 1990 the Congress, which was in effect a parliament for the Russian republic, declared its own sovereignty from the USSR – that is to say, where laws passed by the republic were in conflict with laws of the USSR, the former took precedence over the latter. This sovereignty was not recognised by Gorbachev and was against the terms of the Soviet constitution. The result was a continual struggle between the Soviet institutions and those of the RSFSR and other republics to assert their authority. This period in Russian politics is frequently characterised by two phrases – the 'parade of sovereignties' under which even the small autonomous republics of the RSFSR declared their sovereignty both from the USSR and the RSFSR, and the 'war of laws' in which the Soviet and republican legislatures sought to pass laws in competition with one another.

Gorbachev now faced a serious radical challenge to his own authority, in the form of the liberals who had just about managed to secure a majority in the legislature of the largest republic under Yeltsin's leadership. Subsequently he was faced with pressures from the other direction as the result of a conservative backlash. In June, Gorbachev sanctioned the creation of a Russian Communist Party separate from the CPSU. But the move turned against him when his expressly preferred candidate, the uninspiring Valentin Kuptsov, was defeated in the election to the post of First Secretary by the openly anti-reform Ivan Polozkov. Gorbachev may have seen this development as working to his advantage, as Yeltsin and Polozkov were now left to slug it out in the Russian parliament while Gorbachev stood aloof and ready to exploit the division, a tactic he had used successfully in the past [11: *489*].

But with the traditional power structures of the CPSU undermined, and with the republics moving to escape central control, Gorbachev needed now more than ever to keep on his side the Supreme Soviet of the USSR through which he now governed. While he was quite happy to see liberals and conservatives fight it out in the Russian parliament, in the Supreme Soviet of the USSR the attention of both sides was aimed against Gorbachev himself. Throughout the autumn of 1990 Gorbachev came under constant attack from both the conservatives of the *Soyuz* group and the liberals of the Inter-Regional Group. Gorbachev's fury at the latter's demand that he resign if he failed to implement immediate market reforms may be that which made him determined to throw in his lot with the conservatives [56: *189*], but by then *Soyuz* was the dominant force in the Supreme Soviet anyway. On 1 December the reform-minded Minister of the Interior, Vadim Bakatin, was replaced by the hard-line Boris Pugo, with General Boris Gromov as his deputy. Nikolai Ryzhkov was replaced as Chairman of the Council of Ministers by Valentin Pavlov, and as vice-president of the USSR by Gennadii Yanaev – all of the new appointees were conservatives, who later played a key role in the failed August 1991 coup. A further blow was dealt to the reformers when, against Gorbachev's intentions, Eduard Shevardnadze resigned as Foreign Minister on 20 December.

During this 'conservative turn' on Gorbachev's part, Yeltsin sought to broaden the base of his support by promising to recognise the sovereignty and even independence of the non-Russian republics, by giving his support to the striking miners, and by issuing laws and embarking on economic reform programmes which met with the approval of much of the Russian population. He also appealed openly to Russian national sentiment, forming an alliance with leaders of the Russian Orthodox Church and raising the possibility that Russia would be politically and economically more stable if it broke or weakened its ties with the other republics. In March 1991 a demonstration of 200,000 people in his support in Moscow underlined Yeltsin's popularity. This, combined with his emergence as the spokesperson for most of the republican governments, finally persuaded Gorbachev to make another about turn, aligning himself with Yeltsin and declaring that the pair would be working together from then on in the pursuit of reform, although he did not remove the conservatives from the Soviet government.

The successful referendum on the future of the Union was followed by the assent of the leaders of nine of the republics, marshalled by Yeltsin, to the so-called Novo–Ogarevo agreement which laid out the principles of a new Union Treaty, due to be signed on 20 August.

If at this point the future was looking brighter for Gorbachev, Yeltsin's influence was growing by the day. On 13 June his stock rose further when, in the first elections to the post of Russian President, Yeltsin secured 60 per cent of the popular vote. This gave him greater popular legitimacy than any Russian leader since the seventeenth century. Gorbachev had never submitted himself to a direct popular vote, and opinion polls showed that Yeltsin had surpassed him in popularity already in 1990. Although Gorbachev was, in theory, in the stronger position, his base of support had evaporated: the CPSU was divided and weak, and he had managed to alienate both liberals and conservatives in the USSR Supreme Soviet. Whether he was aware of it or not, any control he could exercise over the republics, following the public relations disaster over Lithuania in January, was entirely dependent on Yeltsin's goodwill.

According to Martin McCauley Yeltsin's decision to join forces with Gorbachev in the spring of 1991 was a cynical manoeuvre which formed part of a plan to eventually overthrow him: 'Yeltsin was playing a waiting game. By signing the Novo–Ogarevo accord, he was ensuring that Gorbachev stayed in office. A weak Gorbachev suited him until he could launch his challenge to destroy him' [56: 211]. Another aspect of Yeltsin's behaviour was also open to cynical interpretations. While he had established firm credentials as a reformer and even a democrat by 1987, his support for Russian nationalism and readiness to countenance the breakup of the USSR was something quite new. Robert Service terms this playing the 'Russian card' [11: 488]. In his account, Yeltsin's personal rivalry with Gorbachev came to play the dominant role in his politics. Excluded from the power structures of the Soviet Union, Yeltsin sought to build up an alternative base in the only other structure available to him – the parliament of the Russian Federation. As a direct result of Yeltsin's quest for power, the last year and a half of the Soviet Union was dominated by an institutional struggle between the USSR and the republics, polarising politics, contributing to the economic crisis, isolating Gorbachev, and leaving only two paths open for the future – the dismantling of communism or a conservative counter-reform which would take the Soviet Union back to the days of Brezhnev and which could only be achieved through the use of force.

The extent to which Yeltsin himself (or, indeed, Gorbachev) was responsible for the final collapse of Soviet communism needs to be considered from the broader perspective of other larger forces which were at work in the Soviet Union in 1989–91. As a prominent and popular leader and an astute politician Yeltsin was unique and came to command a prominent place in 1989–91. But he was not acting alone. The split between conservatives and liberals would have existed without him, and it is hard to see how his influence could have had much impact on the national movements in the Baltic republics, Ukraine and elsewhere, even if the actions of the Russian Federation were key to the ultimate unravelling of the Soviet Union. Finally, it has to be considered whether Gorbachev had simply run out of options, and that the emergence of Yeltsin as a figurehead for liberal reform and democracy was simply a result of him being in the right place at the right time.

17 The August 1991 Coup

Some time on 18 August 1991 a State Emergency Committee was formed in Moscow, including in its numbers Gorbachev's vice president Gennady Yanaev, KGB chairman Vladimir Kryuchkov, Prime Minister Valentin Pavlov, defence minister Dmitrii Yazov, interior minister Boris Pugo, and Gorbachev's trusted chief of staff Valeri Boldin. Among their leading supporters they counted some of the country's top military officials. On the morning of the 19 August, having taken control of all the national newspapers, radio and television stations, the Committee announced that Gorbachev was sick and Yanaev was assuming his powers. Immediately exposing this claim as a lie, they also announced a six month state of emergency, a ban on strikes, demonstrations, opposition political activities, and the subordination of all levels of government to the Committee. Tanks appeared on the streets of Moscow, and a number of prominent liberals were arrested and warrants ordered for the arrest of many more.

At this time Gorbachev was on a working vacation at Foros in the Crimea, putting the finishing touches to the latest version of his new Union Treaty. On 18 August, a high ranking delegation representing the Emergency Committee visited him to secure his approval for the state of emergency and, when this was not forthcoming, effectively put him under house arrest and prevented any communication with the outside world. The tension of the situation apparently caused some kind of nervous breakdown in Gorbachev's wife, Raisa. Gorbachev's was just the first act of defiance out of many, but, crucially, his confinement prevented him from playing any role in the events of the next three days.

Although preparations for the coup had been in progress for some months, it appears to have been poorly planned and even worse in execution. Yeltsin and his vice president, Alexander Rutskoi, were among the numerous targets on the plotters' arrest list who were left at large. While the Russian media was mostly gagged, nothing was done about foreign journalists whose reports were then broadcast back into the USSR. Yanaev did not help the cause by appearing visibly nervous at the Committee's first press conference. Yeltsin and Rutskoi took advantage by setting up camp at the Russian parliamentary building, the White House. They were joined by prominent figures such as the cellist Mstislav Rostropovich, Andrei Sakharov's widow Elena Bonner, the former foreign minister Eduard Shevardnadze and tens of thousands of ordinary Muscovites determined that the coup would not succeed. Demonstrations and strikes broke out across the country, but it was at the White House that resistance was focused. Although three demonstrators lost their lives in clashes with the military elsewhere in Moscow, soldiers who were sent to the White House itself refused to open fire. Crucially, the head of the Soviet airforce, Pavel Grachev, who the plotters had considered to be on their side, came down on Yeltsin's side and far from putting his aircraft at the disposal of the coup, threatened to use them to prevent any helicopter attacks on the White House.

By then splits among the coup organisers were already apparent, with hardliners having to overrule Yanaev, who balked at further military action. But as soon as it became clear that the coup was not going to be an easy *fait accompli*, military commanders one by one adopted a wait and see strategy, leaving the conspirators with no troops at their disposal. After three days defence minister Yazov, too, broke ranks and called off all military action.

By the middle of 21 August the coup was effectively over. A number of leading conspirators flew to Foros to plead directly with Gorbachev – whether for forgiveness, or to come over to their side against Yeltsin, is not clear as Gorbachev refused to meet them. They were soon arrested by Rutskoi, who arrived in Foros not long after, and took his prisoners and the liberated presidential family back to Moscow on the same plane.

The August coup has sometimes been compared with the ouster of Nikita Khrushchev as First Secretary of the CPSU in 1964 [47: 79]. While this might have been at the back of the conspirators' minds, it was a different case altogether: Khrushchev was by then an isolated figure in the Presidium and CC, most of whose members had been carefully prepared and were on the side of the new leaders. While military preparations were in place, this was only as back-up, and Khrushchev was removed by entirely peaceful and legal means. In fact there was no precedent at all for what the conspirators were doing in 1991 in any communist state. This lack of a successful model is part of the explanation for why the coup was so ill-prepared. It was also the reason behind disagreements as to what the real aims of the coup were. The most pressing issue that united conservatives, the military and the KGB was to preserve the integrity of the Soviet Union, and it was the pronouncements on this issue which might have earned the conspirators some public support. The timing of the attempt indicates that its immediate aim was to prevent the signing of the new Union Treaty. One interpretation is that the coup organisers, who included a number of people close to Gorbachev, did not intend to overthrow him, but rather to put pressure on him and encourage him to stand up to Yeltsin and other opponents without fear. The fact that Gorbachev was detained *incommunicado* at Foros rather than arrested or formally deposed suggests that the aim may have been to provide him with a *fait accompli* which would allow him eventually to return to Moscow in a stronger position than he had been before. Others argue that while the aim was, indeed, to replace Gorbachev, the unwillingness to launch an assault on the White House shows that the aim was to achieve a constitutional changeover but that the conspirators had no stomach for bloodshed or plunging the country into a civil war [5: *193*]. On the other hand, the intention to make widespread arrests and the immediate imposition of tight controls on the media suggested the more far-reaching intention of undoing *glasnost* and *perestroika* altogether and returning to something more like the days of Brezhnev.

There is almost as little clarity over the motives of the masses who demonstrated or struck in protest at the takeover. Yeltsin and Rutskoi had nothing to lose and everything to gain by resistance – at very best, a successful coup would mean an end to their political careers, and most likely far worse. But the same could not be said for the 55-year-old woman who declared in front of the White House 'I'll let a tank roll over me if I have to. I'll die right here if I have to' [5: *192*]. What is important yet unclear, given the aftermath of the coup, is the extent to which demonstrators believed they were defending Gorbachev, as opposed to supporting the increasingly popular Yeltsin, or just taking a stand for freedom. Whatever the actual case, it was Yeltsin who succeeded, with some justification given his own role, in claiming the legitimacy which this popular mobilisation conferred. This was the most important consequence of the coup – whether the plan had been to push Gorbachev to a more conservative position or to replace him altogether, the actual outcome was to massively reinforce the standing of his most renowned liberal rival, Boris Yeltsin.

The bungling and lack of foresight involved in the coup and the fact that its leaders were all Gorbachev appointees has given rise to conspiracy theories suggesting that Gorbachev himself was behind the attempt, hoping thereby to present himself as the saviour of the Soviet Union against the forces of reaction. It is more likely that the farcical nature of the coup can be explained by radical miscalculations on the part of the conspirators, based largely on two assumptions which turned out to be completely unfounded: first that the Soviet Union's top military brass would unanimously declare their support for the coup and provide the essential military back-up; and second, that ordinary Russian citizens would stay at home in impassive indifference, particularly in Moscow, the capital city and focal point of the coup attempt.

With the benefit of hindsight, these assumptions look like the result of sheer stupidity. At the time, however, they may have appeared entirely reasonable. The generals and airforce commanders on whom so much depended, had most to lose as a result of the direction in which Gorbachev was taking the country. Unlike in the Brezhnev era, nobody could feel secure in their position: Gorbachev had shown his readiness to stand up to the military and to scapegoat individuals when necessary. This had been amply illustrated in the wake of the Matthias Rust affair (see Chapter 10), and the dressing down Gorbachev had given the generals at that time no doubt still rankled. The consequences of economic crisis had already been felt in the armed forces, with much deeper cuts threatened. The privileged and powerful position of the generals and their allies in the military-industrial complex had been undermined for the first time since Stalin's demotion of the architects of the Red Army's victory in the Second World War. The senior military also shared a common background and set of beliefs which led them to embrace Soviet patriotic values more than any other section of society. The loss of the Soviet Union's Great Power status, the abandonment of the communist regimes in Eastern Europe, and the potential loss of the Baltic and other republics from the USSR were seen as humiliating and unnecessary.

The miners' strikes and other episodes should have warned the conspirators that Russians were no longer prepared to sit passively at home and await whatever fate the country's leaders decided for them. The events of 1989 in East Germany, Czechoslovakia and Romania, or Poland in 1980–81, presented an even starker reminder of the volatility and power of the people. On the other hand, significant manifestations of unrest had been confined to the Russian coalfields and the non-Russian republics. With the exceptions of the sporadic recent pro-Yeltsin demonstrations, Moscow, Leningrad and the other major cities of central Russia had witnessed little in the way of mass street demonstrations or angry mobs since the revolutions of 1917. Most Russians had suffered a profound fall in living standards since Gorbachev came into office, while job security and basic welfare were no longer guaranteed. The loss of international status and the prospect of a dismembered USSR were at odds with the image of greatness with which most Russians had been brought up, or for which they or their parents and grandparents had sacrificed so much in 1941–45. Russians had little to thank Gorbachev for, his popularity had sunk to new depths, and a changing of the guard which promised to restore the much lamented features of the good old days could have been expected at best to evoke widespread support for the coup, at worst to leave the field of conflict to politicians and the military.

The conspirators may have been lulled into a sense of security by deeper considerations. In the early 1980s, western political scientists developed the concept of 'political culture' to explain what they saw as the deeply ingrained characteristics of different peoples. According to such descriptions, for a variety of historical and cultural reasons, Russians were by nature passive, obeisant to whatever authorities were in control at any particular time, and only mobilised into mass action when pushed to the extreme [15]. Czechs and Poles may be sparked into revolt by the slightest of fuses, but their historical experience and collective psychology was altogether different from those of the Russians. While the conspirators would not have read these western works, they would have been very aware of the same historical considerations that had given rise to such theories. Gdansk in 1980 or Prague and Bucharest in 1989 would not have been at the back of their minds but Moscow in 1964, when the Khrushchev ouster failed to provoke a single person onto the streets. Decades of complacent reporting in the internal security reports of the KGB also served to reinforce the impression of a passive and obedient population.

So the plan was quite simple: the conspirators, backed up by the security services and the army, would quickly take control of the key buildings and institutions of Moscow which would rapidly spread across the rest of Russia with minimal resistance. It would be harder to bring the republics under control, but with a firm hand at the helm the threat of more consistent military intervention than Gorbachev had been prepared to countenance would have been enough to bring most areas to heel. Where threats failed, a committed use of military force would soon sweep aside any remaining resistance.

These assumptions foundered on a number of points. Many generals, while not necessarily averse to such actions on principle, displayed little confidence in their outcomes, preferring to remain uncommitted until they could see which way the wind was blowing. The conspirators also failed to account for traditional rivalries between the military and the KGB, the demoralisation and depoliticisation of the Army following the humiliation of Afghanistan and Gorbachev's reorganisations, or the fact that the numerous senior personnel changes since 1987 meant that many senior officers actually owed their promotion to Gorbachev and might therefore be inclined to display loyalty to him [42: 6]. The supposed inability of the Russian people to stand up and be counted is demonstrably based on a number of historical fallacies and inadequate consideration of specific circumstances. Thanks in part to the intervention of Yeltsin and his supporters, the choice facing Russians was not one between Gorbachev and Yanaev, but between democracy and authoritarian rule; not between the 'good old days' and an uncertain economic future, but between freedom and the old days of the GULag and the KGB, restrictions on expression and travel, and the repressive monotony of life under Brezhnev; not between a glorious leader of world communism rivalled only by the US on the international arena and a weak, dismembered state, but between a vain and outdated Empire whose republics and satellites, not to mention nuclear arsenal, were a drain on available resources, and a country reduced to its Russian core, which could prosper once stripped of its spurious, ideologically driven military and economic commitments and where the true Russian character could rediscover itself and develop. True, the Russian people had shown little propensity to put themselves at risk in defence of such values over the past 70 years, but these were different times. *Glasnost*, if nothing else, had opened the eyes of the population to new possibilities, possibilities which had been kept alive by the noble example of Sakharov and others. Exhilarated by their first taste of democracy, if only for a moment, the citizens of Moscow who flocked to the White House felt they had something worth fighting and, if necessary, dying for.

All the same, it seems unlikely that the outcome of the coup was a forgone conclusion. While opposition to the plotters in the Baltic republics was predictable, in a number of other republics, most notably the Kirghiz, leaders prevaricated or indicated clearly enough that they were willing to work with the new leadership. The immediate key to the situation was the military leadership in and around Moscow. Had the initial outcomes of the coup not proved so adverse to the plotters, it is not implausible that sections of the military would have closed ranks behind them. The surprising show of defiance in front of the White House appears to have been what deterred the waverers, so that, in particular, the failure to detain Yeltsin (not to mention his exceptional decisiveness and personal courage at this juncture) was the mistake that ultimately made the coup attempt resemble farce more than the tragedy that it could have led to.

18 The End of Communism

The period between the August coup and the end of 1991 has commonly been portrayed as one of administering the final rites to the Soviet Union, but there was still some way to go. Gorbachev returned to Moscow apparently confident that his authority as leader of the Soviet Union would be restored. But he had, by force of circumstance, played no part in resistance to the coup. It was Yeltsin, who had put his life on the line, who could justifiably claim to be the saviour of democracy in the USSR. He brought Gorbachev before the Russian parliament and subjected him to humiliating interrogation, forcing him to name the members of his government who had plotted to remove him. Gorbachev carried on, even defending socialism and the Communist Party, although he was pressured into standing down as General Secretary of the CPSU in August, while retaining his position as President of the USSR. But Yeltsin was now the effective ruler in Moscow, embarking on his own market reform programme and, on 6 November, he decreed the outright banning of the Communist Party of the Soviet Union, of which he had until recently been a member. This move, although it proved legally unenforceable, finally sealed the fate of Soviet communism, if the coup had not already done so.

For a while, Gorbachev and Yeltsin cooperated on plans for the future of the Union, although Gorbachev became increasingly desperate as he saw all effective power slipping into the hands of the republics, to the extent that he offered to resign the Presidency in Yeltsin's favour if only the latter would save the Union. Yeltsin might have been prevailed on, but was probably dissuaded by the attitude of the Ukrainian President Leonid Kravchuk, who refused to take part in further talks and declined to send a representative to sign a Treaty on the Economic Commonwealth on 18 October.

On 24 November, Yeltsin also refused to sign Gorbachev's Union Treaty.

The Ukrainian referendum for independence on 1 December dealt the final blow to the Soviet Union. With the Baltic and Transcaucasian republics already having left the fold, the departure of the second largest republic would leave only a meaningless rump. Yeltsin met with the Ukrainian and Belarusan leaders on 8 December, when the three agreed to set up a loose Commonwealth of Independent States. Faced with little alternative, at the last minute the Central Asian republics signed up to the treaty, together with Moldova, Armenia and Azerbaijan. In the short term, the Commonwealth of Independent States did not serve as much more than a loose trading organisation and a convenient banner for international sporting competitions (although it continued to exist, and appeared to be taking on a more important role in the region by 2004). In effect, the USSR had split up into fifteen separate and entirely independent states.

Left with no Union to govern, Gorbachev delivered an emotional resignation speech on television on 25 December, and on midnight on 31 December 1991 the Soviet Union passed into history.

Looking back at the events of 1991, few would argue that after the August coup either Soviet communism or the USSR had any possibility of surviving. This was not quite as clear at the time. Not only did Gorbachev struggle desperately to preserve something of a continuity, albeit having discarded the label 'communist', US President George Bush snr encouraged the preservation of some sort of Union in the interests of regional stability [12: *483*]. Certainly there was no way back for the conservative communist forces after the coup, and the independence of the Baltic states was inevitable. But the fate of the Soviet Union may have hinged ultimately on the unpredictable attitude of Ukraine, and on the stance of Yeltsin. As long as the battle to preserve the Soviet Union was linked to the question of who would enjoy the greater political authority, Gorbachev or Yeltsin, there was only going to be one outcome. But this perspective, which again emphasises the role of Yeltsin, underlines the possibility that the fate of Soviet communism and of the USSR may have rested on short-term contingent factors rather than the inexorable forces of history.

19 Conclusion

This account has emphasised those factors which may have contributed to the fall of Soviet communism in the short term: an economy spiralling out of control from 1989, the inconsistencies and prevarications of Gorbachev's reform programme, the tactics of nationalist politicians and Boris Yeltsin, the disruption caused by striking workers and mass demonstrations and the fateful actions of the coup organisers. Even chance events like the Chernobyl accident or the Armenian earthquake, both of which might have occurred at any time, and the somewhat deranged behaviour of a young German pilot, all had roles to play in the unfolding of events. These occurrences need to be considered alongside the broader factors such as long-term economic stagnation, social change, loss of ideological legitimacy and national grievances.

But rarely has a case been made for attributing predominance to one factor over any other. Indeed, specialists sometimes appear keener to argue what was not responsible rather than to say what was. Paradoxically, we have seen how the economist Phil Hanson ascribes the Soviet collapse mostly to political factors connected to rivalry between the national republics [22: *227–36, 253–4*], while the expert on Soviet nationalities, Ronald Suny, blames economic decline for both the fall of communism and the national break up of the USSR [34: *121–2*, 12: *453*]. A likewise puzzling, but more explicable, difference exists between political scientists on the one hand, who tend to emphasise the role of longer term historical factors, and historians on the other hand, who frequently place more stress on chance and personality in their accounts.

Suny does at least offer a definite opinion on the reasons for the fall of Soviet communism: he attributes the crises of 1989–91 directly to Gorbachev's attempt to simultaneously democratise the political system, reform the economy and decolonise the republics: 'Had reform begun earlier, or economic conditions been more fortuitous, or the reforms been carried out sequentially, as in China, with economic changes preceding political changes, rather than happening simultaneously, perhaps perestroika might have had a different outcome' [12: *484*]. But the Soviet Union was not China, and there is a strong case to be made that economic reform could not be achieved without overcoming the resistance of the Soviet bureaucracy and exposing the Soviet population to the truth about the defects of the existing system, with all the further consequences implied by *glasnost* [8: *414–15*].

Few other historians have been as bold as to state definitively whether a different course of action might have saved the Soviet Union. Instead, debate has centred around the more general question of long- vs. short-term factors. Alexander Dallin summarises the six long-term factors which may have contributed to the failure of Soviet communism, all of which have been touched on here: (1) the loosening of state control after Stalin's death, and even more under Gorbachev; (2) the spread of corruption; (3) the declining effectiveness of Marxist–Leninist ideology; (4) a changing social structure in which the population was becoming more educated and professionalised; (5) exposure to western influences, in particular the ideas of human rights promoted by Soviet dissidents; (6) relative economic decline [1].

But even Dallin does not conclude from this that the Soviet collapse was inevitable. None of these factors came to the fore until the later part of Gorbachev's rule. Crucially, there were no signs that the population was ready to mobilise in support of change, the dissident movement was tiny, and the economy, while falling further behind the West, was continuing to grow in the mid-80s and could at least satisfy basic needs [5: *83*]. Other attempts to relate an inevitable collapse to long-term systemic weaknesses have never proceeded beyond a level of generalisation and abstract inference, often with political undertones, which have never succeeded in making a convincing case – this is not to say such interpretations must be wrong, but there has not been sufficient work carried out to demonstrate to any level of satisfaction the connection between these long-term factors and the actual unfolding of events in the late 1980s and early 1990s. Where a convincing case for systemic weakness has been made, as with the incompatibility of the changing

110

social structure with the opportunities offered by the communist system, it has still to be shown that the social groups trapped in this dilemma were the prime movers in the fall of Soviet communism.

As more research is carried out, the link between long-term factors and short-term events may be more successfully explored. But for now, we are obliged to pay close attention to the fall of communism as it actually occurred, and in particular to the period following the change of leadership in 1985. Gorbachev and Yeltsin clearly loom large in the process. At a number of critical junctures, Gorbachev made decisions which could have contributed to his own undoing – showing insensitivity to ethnic and national feelings, weakening the CPSU without securing an alternative power base from which to conduct reforms and failing to commit to a consistent economic reform programme [8: *416*] are all examples of how Gorbachev might have handled things differently. Alienating Yeltsin may have been another major mistake, as the combination of the latter's determination, ambition, and resentment, with his charisma and popular appeal made him a unique vehicle for radicalism and, eventually, nationalism.

But Gorbachev and Yeltsin were not working in isolation. From the conservatives and reformers in the Politburo, through the opportunist republican leaders and dissidents, down to the street-level activists, miners and campaigners for environmental, national and human rights, the actors involved in the Soviet demise are too numerous to be accounted for individually. And after all, as Jerry Hough has pointed out [41: *55–8*] even Gorbachev and Yeltsin themselves emerged from the milieu of a generation of post-Stalin communists who had quite different attitudes to the Brezhnev generation and who were already dominant in many of the regions of the Soviet Union.

Yet it is difficult to discern any compelling and unavoidable reasons in existence before 1985, or even before 1989, to explain why these forces should come together in such a way so as to bring about the end of Soviet communism, and it is hard to identify any groups which were actively working towards such an end. The Baltic national movements, perhaps, but for them the question of democracy and market reform was almost secondary to the issue of independence. And they were not, on their own, powerful enough to bring the whole edifice crashing down. Other groups – dissidents, workers, liberal reformers, shared many features of what eventually became Gorbachev's vision and rarely posed any direct threat to the system.

In their work on the destruction of the Soviet economic system published in 1998, Michael Ellman and Vladimir Kontorovich claimed 'At the moment we are at the stage in which the most varied explanations are being offered but little is being done to test them' [71: *3*]. Not much progress has been made in the six years since. The complexity of the overlap of a number of different factors presents some problems to arriving at a definitive conclusion as to why communism collapsed. Vague attempts at 'modelling' – determining what would have happened if one or other factor was removed from the equation – for example, have so far proved unpromising. Political scientists, who have dominated the literature on the Gorbachev period to date, tend to start from an overarching explanation in the form of a theory or model. While these can be useful in setting out the framework of future investigation, and have generated several plausible hypotheses, they are not a sufficient substitute for detailed empirical examination of the facts. At a distance of more than a decade, it is now perhaps time to combine existing detailed studies with basic research of the national and local political situation from whatever sources are available, building a picture of events from the bottom-up. This is one respect in which historical study has a distinct advantage over political science. The possibility of conducting extensive oral history, (of which Ellman and Kontorovich provide one example at the elite level), and the relative richness of published newspaper and other sources when compared to the earlier Soviet period, should make this a tempting period to study. Easier access to archived materials from the late 1980s, particularly those of the leading bodies of the CPSU, would greatly enhance the prospects for a detailed historical approach.

Given the current state of historical study, no conclusive answer can be given to the question of why Soviet communism fell. The complexity of events between 1985 and 1991, of which this account has provided a greatly simplified version, combined with the absence of any convincing demonstration of the inevitability of the fall of communism, suggests that short-term factors played a crucial role, though readers may have their own views as to which should be accorded most prominence. At least, investigation of the last years of the Soviet Union, while it may not explain precisely *why* Soviet communism fell, should illuminate *how* it fell in the way it did.

Chronology of Events, 1985–91

1985

10 March	Death of Konstantin Chernenko, General Secretary of the CPSU.
11 March	Mikhail Gorbachev becomes General Secretary of the CPSU.
7 April	Gorbachev declares unilateral moratorium on deployment of SS-20 missiles in Europe.
23 April	Nikolai Ryzhkov, Yegor Ligachev and Viktor Chebrikov are promoted to full membership of the Politburo.
17 May	Anti-alcohol campaign launched.
1 July	Grigorii Romanov is removed from the Politburo.
2 July	Andrei Gromyko made Chairman of the Presidium of the USSR Supreme Soviet.
19–21 November	Gorbachev meets US President Ronald Reagan at Geneva Summit.
23 November	Five agricultural ministries merged to form *Gosagroprom*.

1986

15 January	Gorbachev proposes 3-stage programme of complete nuclear disarmament.
8 February	Gorbachev criticises Andrei Sakharov in French newspaper L'Humanité.
25–26 February	27th Congress of the CPSU. Changes in the composition of the Politburo. Gorbachev expresses criticisms of the Brezhnev era.
26 April	Major explosion at Chernobyl nuclear plant in Ukraine.
June	Conflicts between Yakuts and Russians in Yakutia.

June	*Glavlit* and the Union of Writers relax rules on censorship.
16 June	12th Five Year Plan inaugurated.
22 September	CSCE Conference on Confidence and Security Building Measures in Stockholm.
11–12 October	Reykjavik summit fails to reach agreement on disarmament.
16 December	Dinmukhamed Kunaev is replaced by Gennadii Kolbin as First Secretary of the Kazakhstan Communist Party, sparking off two days of rioting in Almaty.
16 December	Gorbachev telephones dissident Andrei Sakharov and invites him to return to Moscow from internal exile.

1987

13 January	Law on Joint Ventures.
28 January	Alexander Yakovlev promoted to candidate member of the Politburo.
3 February	Brezhnev's son-in-law Yurii Churbanov charged with corruption.
29 May	German pilot Mathias Rust lands a light aircraft in Red Square.
30 May	Sergei Sokolov dismissed as Defence Minister.
21 June	First multicandidate elections for a small number of local soviets.
1 July	Law on the State Enterprise.
8 July	Police charge protesting Crimean Tatars in Moscow.
September	Yeltsin writes to Gorbachev asking to be relieved of his posts as head of the Moscow City Party organisation and candidate member of the Politburo.
21 October	Yeltsin attacks Ligachev in front of the Central Committee of the CPSU.
11 November	Yeltsin dismissed as head of Moscow City Party organisation.
10 December	Gorbachev and Reagan sign Intermediate Nuclear Forces Treaty in Washington.

1988

January	Soviet withdrawal from Afghanistan announced.
February	Club for the Democratisation of Trade Unions formed.
18 February	Yeltsin dismissed from Politburo.
20 February	Unofficial referendum in Nagorno–Karabakh shows support for joining to Armenia. Mass demonstrations in Armenia.

28 February	More than 30 Armenians massacred in Sumgait.
13 March	*Sovetskaia Rossiia* publishes Nina Andreeva's letter.
April	Popular Front formed in Estonia.
5 April	Politburo response to the Andreeva letter, written by Yakovlev, published in *Pravda*.
May	Sajudis formed in Lithuania.
7 May	Five members of Democratic Forum arrested in Moscow.
26 May	Law on Cooperatives.
June	Popular Front formed in Latvia.
28 June	19th All-Union Conference of the CPSU opens.
4–8 July	General strike and demonstrations in Armenia.
30 September	Gromyko retires as Chairman of the Presidium of the USSR Supreme Soviet.
1 October	Supreme Soviet elects Gorbachev President of the USSR.
22 November	Mass demonstrations and ethnic conflict in Baku, leading to declaration of a State of Emergency in the city and the imposition of direct rule from Moscow over Nagorno Karabakh.
7 December	Earthquake in Armenia kills 25,000.

1989

15 February	Last Soviet troops leave Afghanistan.
26 March	Elections to the USSR Congress of Peoples Deputies.
9 April	Troops fire on demonstrators in Georgian capital Tbilisi.
25 April	Withdrawal of Soviet troops from Eastern Europe begins in Hungary.
18 May	Lithuanian Supreme Soviet declares sovereignty.
25 May	USSR Congress of Peoples Deputies convenes.
27 May	Yeltsin wins seat in Supreme Soviet of the USSR.
July	Miners strike in Siberia, Kuzbass, Vorkuta, Donbass and Kazakhstan.
July	State Commission on Economic Reform created under Leonid Abalkin.
8 July	Gorbachev rejects the 'Brezhnev doctrine'.
30 July	Sakharov, Yeltsin and others form the Inter-Regional Group of deputies in the Congress of Peoples Deputies.
23 August	A human chain of over a million people stretches for 400 miles across the Baltic republics.
27 October	Miners strike in Vorkuta.
14 December	Andrei Sakharov dies.
16 December	Ryzhkov announces a two year delay in initiating the economic reform programme in the USSR.

1990

January	MVD troops mobilised against demonstrations in Moscow.
11 January	Gorbachev visits Vilnius and denounces independence movement.
13–14 January	Armenians massacred in Azerbaijan.
20 January	Red Army occupies Baku.
4 February	250,000 join a mass rally in Moscow calling for an end to the CPSU's constitutional monopoly of power.
7 February	Central Committee of CPSU supports ending of political monopoly.
24 February	Sajudis wins free elections in Lithuania.
4 March	Yeltsin elected to Supreme Soviet of the RSFSR and becomes its Chairman.
11 March	Lithuanian Supreme Soviet declares independence from USSR.
15 March	Supreme Soviet of the USSR elects Gorbachev as President.
25 March	Paratroopers occupy headquarters of Lithuanian Communist Party.
30 March	Estonian Supreme Soviet declares independence from USSR.
4 May	Latvian Supreme Soviet declares independence from USSR.
16 May	Congress of Peoples Deputies of the RSFSR meets.
24 May	Ryzhkov proposes radical economic reforms.
8 June	Congress of Peoples Deputies of the RSFSR declares sovereignty.
11 July	One-day miners' strike.
11 July	Ligachev loses in election to become Gorbachev's deputy in the CPSU.
9 October	RSFSR adopts Shatalin's 500 day plan for economic reform.
15 October	Gorbachev awarded Nobel Prize for Peace.
23 November	Gorbachev announces draft of a new Union Treaty for the USSR.
20 December	Eduard Shevardnadze resigns as Foreign Minister.

1991

1 January	Some prices liberalised.
7 January	Paratroopers enter all three Baltic republics.
13 January	Paratroopers storm TV Tower in Vilnius, killing 14.
10 March	200,000 demonstrate in Moscow in support of Yeltsin.

17 March	Referendum on the preservation of the USSR shows overwhelming support.
March–May	Miners strike across the Soviet Union.
23 April	Yeltsin and other republican leaders endorse new Union Treaty.
13 June	Yeltsin elected President of the RSFSR with 60 per cent of the popular vote.
July	Strategic Arms Reduction Treaty (START) signed in Moscow.
18 August	State Emergency Committee formed in Moscow. Gorbachev placed under house arrest in Foros.
19 August	Tanks on the streets of Moscow. Yeltsin and Rutskoi go to the White House.
21 August	Coup collapses. Gorbachev returns to Moscow and steps down as leader of the CPSU while retaining the presidency.
6 November	Yeltsin bans the CPSU. Ruled unconstitutional.
24 November	Yeltsin refuses to sign Union Treaty.
1 December	Referendum in Ukraine supports independence.
8 December	Leaders of the Russian Federation, Ukraine and Belorussia agree on the formation of the Commonwealth of Independent States.
25 December	Gorbachev resigns as President of the USSR.
31 December	The USSR is formally dissolved.

Glossary of Terms and Abbreviations

CC	Central Committee – formally the leading body of the CPSU
CIS	Commonwealth of Independent States – loose successor to the USSR, excluding the Baltic states
CPD	Congress of People's Deputies – the Soviet parliament from 1989
CPSU	Communist Party of the Soviet Union
CSCE	Commission on Security and Cooperation in Europe
dacha	Weekend/country cottage
demokratizatsiia	Democratisation
DemRossiya	Democratic Russia – the main liberal grouping in the Russian Congress of People's Deputies
FNPR	Federation of Independent Trade Unions of the RSFSR
glasnost	Openness – one of Gorbachev's key policies
Glavlit	Main Administration for Affairs of Literature and Publishing Houses
Gorkom	City Committee (of the CPSU)
Gosplan	State Planning Commission – the main agency responsible for drawing up targets and allocations for the Soviet 5-year plans
GULag	Main Administration of Camps – Stalin's system of Labour Camps
INF Treaty	Intermediate Nuclear Forces Treaty – signed in 1987
IRG	Inter-Regional Group – a group of liberal deputies, including Andrei Sakharov and Boris Yeltsin, in the CPD of the Soviet Union
KGB	Committee of State Security – the Soviet secret police
kolkhozy	Collective Farms
MVD	Ministry of Internal Affairs – responsible for internal security
neformaly	Informal groups – any club or association operating outside of official state or Party structures in the Gorbachev period

Glossary of Terms and Abbreviations

nomenklatura	List of names – a list of senior positions whose appointment was controlled by the CPSU
perestroika	Restructuring – designates economic reform policies, or the period of Gorbachev's reforms in general
Politburo	Political Bureau – the highest permanent body of the CPSU
RSFSR	Russian Socialist Federal Soviet Republic – later the Russian Federation
Sajudis	A Lithuanian nationalist party
SDI	Strategic Defense Initiative, the USA's so-called 'Star Wars' satellite defense programme
Sotsprof	Union of Socialist Trade Unions
sovkhozy	State farms
Soyuz	Union – conservative group in the CPD of the Soviet Union
SSR	Soviet Socialist Republic – used in the title of the non-Russian Republics of the USSR
START	Strategic Arms Reduction Treaty – signed in 1991
Supreme Soviet	The highest law-making body in the Soviet Union
uskorenie	Acceleration – the speeding up of economic growth
USSR	Union of Soviet Socialist Republics – the full title of the Soviet Union

Select Bibliography

This list consists of all the works cited in the text, together with a selection of other relevant works, and includes a number of memoirs which may be useful in supplementing scholarly readings. The list is restricted to English-language works. For ease of use, the bibliography is organised under three main headings: (A) works which look at the collapse of Soviet communism from a broader historical perspective; (B) works dealing with the whole Soviet period, or a part of the Soviet period, but without a specific focus on the years 1985–91; (C) works dealing specifically or mostly with the Gorbachev period, 1985–91. Many works listed in Section B also include extensive coverage of the Gorbachev period. Sections B and C are further arranged according to different topics.

A. The Soviet Collapse in Historical Perspective

[1]   A. Dallin, 'Causes of the collapse of the USSR', *Post-Soviet Affairs* 8:4 (1992).
[2]   R. V. Daniels, *The End of the Communist Revolution* (1993).
[3]   C. Merridale and C. Ward (eds), *Perestroika: The Historical Perspective* (1991).
[4]   R. Pipes, *Communism: a History of the Intellectual and Political Movement* (2001).
[5]   R. Strayer, *Why did the Soviet Union Collapse? Understanding Historical Change* (1998).
[6]   S. White, *Communism and its Collapse* (2001).

B. The Soviet Period

General Histories of Russia and the Soviet Union

[7]   M. Haynes, *Russia: Class and Power 1917–2000* (2002).

120

[8] J. L. H. Keep, *Last of the Empires: A History of the Soviet Union 1945–1991* (1995).

[9] M. Malia, *The Soviet Tragedy: A History of Socialism in Russia, 1917–1991* (1994).

[10] D. Moon, 'The problem of social stability in Russia, 1598–1998', in G. Hosking and R. Service (eds), *Reinterpreting Russia* (1999).

[11] R. Service, *A History of Twentieth Century Russia* (1997).

[12] R. G. Suny, *The Soviet Experiment: Russia, the USSR, and the Successor States* (1998).

[13] D. Volkogonov, *The Rise and Fall of the Soviet Empire: Political Leaders from Lenin to Gorbachev* (1999).

The Soviet Union before Gorbachev

[14] S. Baron, *Bloody Saturday in the Soviet Union: Novocherkassk 1962* (2001).

[15] A. Brown (ed.), *Political Culture and Political Change in Communist States* (1979).

[16] G. Gill, *Stalinism* (1990).

[17] E. Mawdsley, 'An elite within an elite: Politburo/Presidium membership under Stalin, 1927–1953', in E. A. Rees (ed.), *The Nature of Stalin's Dicatatorship: The Politburo, 1924–1953* (2004).

[18] E. A. Rees (ed.), *The Nature of Stalin's Dictatorship: The Politburo, 1924–1953* (2004).

[19] L. Schapiro, *The Communist Party of the Soviet Union* (1960).

Society

[20] D. Lane, *The Rise and Fall of State Socialism* (1996).

The Economy

[21] R. W. Davies, *Soviet Economic Development from Lenin to Khrushchev* (1998).

[22] P. Hanson, *The Rise and Fall of the Soviet Economy* (2003).

[23] M. Harrison, 'Economic growth and slowdown', in E. Bacon and M. Sandle (eds), *Brezhnev Reconsidered* (2002).

[24] M. Harrison, 'Soviet economic growth since 1928: the alternative statistics of G.I.Khanin', *Europe-Asia Studies*, 45 (1993).

[25] A. Nove, *An Economic History of the USSR* (1969).

[26] E. A. Rees, *Centre-Local Relations in the Stalinist State, 1928–1941* (2002).

The Nationalities Question

[27] A. L. Altstadt, *The Azerbaijani Turks: Power and Identity under Russian Rule* (1992).

[28] B. Fowkes, *The Disintegration of the Soviet Union: A Study in the Rise and Triumph of Nationalism* (1997).

[29] R. Karklins, *Ethnic Relations in the USSR* (1986).

[30] T. Martin, *The Affirmative Action Empire: Nations and Nationalism in the Soviet Union, 1923–1939* (2001).

[31] B. Nahaylo and V. Swoboda, *Soviet Disunion: A History of the Nationalities Problem in the USSR* (1990).

[32] R. Pipes, *The Formation of the Soviet Union: Communism and Nationalism, 1917–1923* (1954).

[33] G. Simon, *Nationalism and Policy towards the Nationalities in the Soviet Union* (1991).

[34] R. G. Suny, *The Revenge of the Past: Nationalism, Revolution and the Collapse of the Soviet Union* (1993).

[35] V. Tishkov, *Ethnicity, Nationalism and Conflict in and after the Soviet Union: the Mind Aflame* (1997).

International Relations

[36] R. Garthoff, *The Great Transition: American–Soviet Relations and the End of the Cold War* (1994).

[37] R. C. Nation, *Black Earth, Red Star: A History of Soviet Security Policy, 1917–1991* (1992).

[38] C. Pursiainen, *Russian Foreign Policy and International Relations Theory* (2000).

C. The Gorbachev Period

General

[39] A. d'Agostino, *Gorbachev's Revolution* (1998).

[40] M. Haynes, 'The political economy of the Russian Question after the fall', *Historical Materialism* 10: 4 (2002).

[41] J. F. Hough, *Democratization and Revolution in the USSR, 1985–1991* (1997).

[42] W. Suraska, *How the Soviet Union Disappeared: An Essay on the Causes of Dissolution* (1998).

[43] E. Walker, *Dissolution: Sovereignty and the Break-up of the Soviet Union* (2003).

[44] S. White, *After Gorbachev* (1993).

Select Bibliography

Journalistic Accounts

[45]   D. Remnick, *Lenin's Tomb: The Last Days of the Soviet Empire* (1993).

[46]   A. Roxburgh, *The Second Russian Revolution* (1991).

[47]   J. Steele, *Eternal Russia: Yeltsin, Gorbachev and the Mirage of Democracy* (1994).

Memoirs

[48]   V. Boldin, *Ten Years that Shook the World: The Gorbachev Era as Witnessed by his Chief of Staff* (1994).

[49]   M. Gorbachev, *Memoirs* (1995).

[50]   Y. Ligachev, *Inside Gorbachev's Kremlin* (1993).

[51]   E. Shevardnadze, *The Future Belongs to Freedom* (1991).

[52]   B. Yeltsin, *Against the Grain. An Autobiography* (1990).

Works on Gorbachev and Yeltsin

[53]   L. Aron, *Boris Yeltsin: A Revolutionary Life* (2000).

[54]   A. Brown, *The Gorbachev Factor* (1996).

[55]   G. W. Breslauer, *Gorbachev and Yeltsin as Leaders* (2002).

[56]   M. McCauley, *Gorbachev* (1998).

[57]   J. Morrison, *Boris Yeltsin: From Bolshevik to Democrat* (1991).

Politics

[58]   N. Andreyeva, 'I cannot forgo my principles', in A. Dallin and G. W. Lapidus (eds), *The Soviet System: From Crisis to Collapse* (1995).

[59]   F. Benvenuti, 'Reforming the party: organisation and structure 1917–1990', in C. Merridale and C. Ward (eds), *Perestroika: The Historical Perspective* (1991).

[60]   A. Brown, 'Political change in the Soviet Union', in A. Dallin and G. W. Lapidus (eds), *The Soviet System: From Crisis to Collapse* (1995).

[61]   C. Merridale, 'Perestroika and political pluralism: past and prospects', in C. Merridale and C. Ward (eds), *Perestroika: the Historical Perspective* (1991).

Society

[62]   J. Aves, 'The Russian labour movement, 1989–91: a Russian Solidarnosc?', in G. A. Hosking, J. Aves and P. J. S. Duncan (eds),

The Road to Post-Communism: Independent Political Movements in the Soviet Union 1985–1991 (1992).

[63]   M. Buckley (ed.), *Perestroika and Soviet Women* (1992).

[64]   D. Filtzer, *Soviet Workers and the Collapse of Perestroika* (1994).

[65]   G. Hosking, 'The beginnings of independent political activity', in G. A. Hosking, J. Aves and P. J. S. Duncan (eds), *The Road to Post-Communism: Independent Political Movements in the Soviet Union 1985–1991* (1992).

[66]   D. Lane, 'The roots of political reform: The changing social structure of the USSR', in C. Merridale and C. Ward (eds), *Perestroika: The Historical Perspective* (1991).

[67]   D. Lane, *Soviet Economy and Society* (1985).

The Economy

[68]   A. Agenbegyan, *The Economic Challenge of Perestroika* (1988).

[69]   A. Åslund, *Gorbachev's Struggle for Economic Reform* (1989).

[70]   M. Bradshaw, P. Hanson and D. Shaw, 'Economic restructuring', in G. Smith (ed.), *The Baltic States: The National Self-Determination of Estonia, Latvia and Lithuania* (1994).

[71]   M. Ellman and V. Kontorovich (eds), *The Destruction of the Soviet Economic System: An Insider's History* (1998).

[72]   M. Harrison, 'Coercion, compliance and the collapse of the Soviet command economy', *Economic History Review* 55: 3 (2002).

[73]   J. F. Hough, 'The Gorbachev reform: a maximal case', in E. A. Hewett and V. H. Winston (eds), *Milestones in Glasnost and Perestroika: the Economy* (1991).

[74]   J. H. Noren, 'The economic crisis: another perspective', in E. A. Hewett and V. H. Winston (eds), *Milestones in Glasnost and Perestroika: The Economy* (1991).

The Nationalities Question

[75]   I. Bremmer, 'Post-Soviet nationalities theory: past, present, and future', in I. Bremmer and R. Taras (eds), *New States, New Politics: Building the Post-Soviet Nations* (1997).

[76]   T. Colton and R. H. Legvold (eds), *After the Soviet Union: From Empire to Nations* (1992).

[77]   J. D. Fearon, 'Commitment problems and the spread of ethnic conflict', in D. A. Lake and D. Rothchild (eds), *The International Spread of Ethnic Conflict* (1998).

[78]   S. F. Jones, 'Georgia: the trauma of statehood', in I. Bremmer and R. Taras (eds), *New States, New Politics: Building the Post-Soviet Nations* (1997).

[79]   G. W. Lapidus, 'Gorbachev's nationalities problem', in A. Dallin and G. W. Lapidus (eds), *The Soviet System: From Crisis to Collapse* (1995).

[80]   G. W. Lapidus, 'The impact of perestroika on the national question', in G. W. Lapidus, V. Zaslavsky and P. Goldman (eds), *From Union to Commonwealth: Nationalism and Separatism in the Soviet Republics* (1992).

[81]   A. Motyl, 'From imperial decay to imperial collapse: the fall of the Soviet Empire in comparative perspective', in R. Rudolph and D. Good (eds), *Nationalism and Empire: The Habsburg Empire and the Soviet Union* (1992).

[82]   M. B. Olcott, 'Kazakhstan: pushing for Eurasia', in I. Bremmer and R. Taras (eds), *New States, New Politics: Building the Post-Soviet Nations* (1997).

[83]   G. Smith, 'The resurgence of nationalism', in G. Smith (ed.), *The Baltic States: The National Self-Determination of Estonia, Latvia and Lithuania* (1994).

[84]   C. Tilly, 'How empires end', in K. Barkey and M. von Hagen (eds), *After Empire: Multiethnic Societies and Nation-Building – the Soviet Union and the Russian, Ottoman and Habsburg Empires* (1997).

[85]   C. J. Walker, *Armenia and Karabagh: The Struggle for Unity* (1991).

[86]   V. Zaslavsky, 'The Soviet Union', in K. Barkey and M. von Hagen (eds), *After Empire: Multiethnic Societies and Nation-Building – the Soviet Union and the Russian, Ottoman and Habsburg Empires* (1997).

Index

Index

Index

Index